AUTHOR PRAISE

The Pinstripe Prisoner is a well-crafted book that wastes no time engaging the reader in a strong storyline that moves easily between South Africa and the United Kingdom. It portrays characters whose flaws, hopes and dreams are those experienced by us all as we go about the business of our daily lives, maintaining the superficial masks and personas that are all too commonplace in today's modern world. Characters are developed with skill, each one gradually revealing diverse traits and backgrounds that add to the emotional depth and complexity of the novel. One of the strengths of this book is its momentum, which is sustained by its well-paced plot development. Action is quickly framed by the brutality, injustice and racial inequities that characterise post-apartheid South Africa specifically and the rest of the world in general. The novel is constructed with balance and a consistent sense of purpose. The writing style is direct and does not stray from the central premise of the book. The author is to be commended for writing an eloquent book of thought-provoking relevance. It left this reader waiting for the next chapter …
    Margaret Wick, Judge, *The Society of Women Writers NSW Book Awards – The Pinstripe Prisoner: Winner of The Society of Women Writers NSW Fiction Award 2022.*

At turns insightful, disturbing and wrenching. *The Pinstripe Prisoner* is a deeply psychological portrait of one young man's attempt to cope with a horrific event and its aftermath. While the present moves at a catastrophic speed, the narrator's touching memories allow the reader to pause, reflect and find peace.
    Judge's comments, Yeovil Literary Prize

This collection has a timeless message that lends itself to the current generation ... painting a picture of a fierce warrior who is both strong and protective, an advocate of fairness when there's none and a multicoloured messenger of truth and hope worthy of any urban wall.

Dannielle Line, Author and Editor

Kelly Van Nelson's website is titled with the description: EDGY STORIES FROM INSIDE THE MIND. I find this an apt description of her poetry. It's very edgy, an unfiltered musing on the darker elements present within society. The hidden, the insidious, the things people want to hide from. Her prose is powerful and rather impressive. Kelly Van Nelson is a talent to watch for those interested in the Australian poetry scene.

Theresa Smith Writes

This book is packed with heavy themes and raw, unfiltered poetry that speaks directly to the poet's experience of violence, abuse and bullying. The author's working-class upbringing informs her perspective, lingering in the corners of most poems, sometimes with nostalgia and sometimes with powerful, bitter resonance.

Holden Sheppard, Author

This poet's work began with themes gathered in her early days as an underdog on a council estate in Newcastle upon Tyne. Using simple powerful language, she offers the reader a very personal perspective about life on the gritty side. With honesty and heart, Van Nelson tackles concerns such as discrimination, corporate and playground bullying, domestic violence, mental illness and other important social justice issues. Her collection speaks of hard yards and heartbreak, but there is also a sense of hope and courage.

Writing WA

To keep your truth in sight you must keep yourself in sight, and the world should be a mirror to reflect your image and to reflect upon. This is exactly what Kelly Van Nelson conveys. It is her journey, the good, the bad and the ugly. By putting it to paper she turns her experiences into a way to bounce back from her underdog world and help others in the process. We are thrilled to have her collection of poetry in our Hollywood Swag Bags honouring Oscar Weekend.

Lisa Gal Bianchi

The beauty of poetry: when it is written exceptionally well it takes you to a place of vulnerability. It gets your heart beating and your thoughts branching out to question, to wonder, to connect, to understand, to break the barriers of judgement. Kelly Van Nelson is one such poet that takes you one step further than this, diving into a world that hits so many relevant topics in today's world. It's not just poetry. It's hardcore magic. This masterpiece touched my soul.

Mickey Martin, Author

Graffiti Lane swaps rose-coloured glasses for grit, dirt and shadow. There's a rawness and simplicity to the language that evokes feelings of empathy, 'I've-been-there' understanding, empowerment, sadness, tenderness and even smiles. One minute you're wincing and the next you're nodding your head – it's that kind of poetry; poetry that gets people, that reveals the poet's heart, poetry that packs a punch.

Monique Mulligan, Author

Poetically written, the rawness of the words immediately drew me in from the first page. Written in an utterly honest fashion, Kelly Van

Nelson skilfully explores both the darker side of human nature, as well as the hope and resilience within every one of us. Profoundly moving and emotionally charged, I loved reading it.

Yu Dan Shi, Author of Come Alive

Great collection of poems showcasing deep insight into the human psyche as it deals with life's challenges. The author has a natural talent of capturing the raw feelings and artistically playing it back in beautiful language. Highly recommended for anyone interested in diving into life's emotional roller-coaster.

Omar Alim

A well-written and thought-provoking book that leaves the reader reflecting on the emotional intensity of the words and message relayed through them. Highly recommended.

Danielle Aitken, Author

This collection of urban poetry is just incredible. Sometimes challenging to read, because of the emotions it invokes or the fact you think on it for a while. Some beautiful moments too. The author has an incredible voice and her works in this book have something for everyone.

Jacie Anderson, Author

Dark and distressing themes are laid bare, yet accomplished poet Kelly Van Nelson manages to imbue a sense of hope, rather than hopelessness, approaching every topic with unwavering honesty, unafraid to venture into harrowing territory to reflect on a myriad of challenges. Using the vernacular of the street, the boardroom and the domestic front, Van Nelson reveals a keen sensory perceptiveness, an acute awareness of injustice, a deep-rooted empathy and the life-altering potential of resilience.

Maureen Eppen, Author and Blogger

This collection provides a raw, eclectic mix of poems relating to many of today's issues. What I liked most about it is the accessibility of the writing, which is understandable and highly emotive.

Lisa Wolstenholme, Author

Graffiti Lane is an engaging collection of poems that revolve around the concept of being the underdog, bullying and finding ways to bounce back. The poet's angst and fear will help readers perceive the broader effects of discrimination and bullying as they bleed into teenage bullying, corporate bullying and harassment, gender inequality, domestic violence and suicide. The poems are raw, dark and intense and will take readers to a dimension where they realise that there is always hope.

Mamta Madhavan for Readers' Favorite

Punch and Judy explores the horrors of relationship breakdown in graphic detail, yet, for me, anyway, it was not so much a horror story as one of growth and resilience. Even in her darkest moments, 'Judy' asserts her right to be; she is an everywoman, a heroine who we feel deeply for, willing her on and applauding her efforts to extricate herself from the toxicity in which she finds herself enmired. A rollicking tale in verse, with an economy of words that really pack a punch with every line. Make yourself a big pot of coffee, sit down and enjoy the ride!

Julia Kaylock, Poet

What a ride *Rolling in the Mud* is, from the sly humour of a cheeky widower getting payback to the desperation of bullying and abuse, this collection takes you through the gamut of emotions. I had intended to pace myself and read just a couple of stories at a time and instead found myself reading it all in one day. Thoroughly enjoyed it and well recommended.

Karyl Treble

I am such a huge fan of this authoress! *Retrospection* is full of spunk and grit. I couldn't get enough of it. Loved each one! A must-add to your bookshelf and makes a sensational gift to those who welcome adventure in short bursts of poetry.

Rosa Carrafa Publishing

Punch and Judy is an expressive, hard-hitting and intense form of contemporary poetry from Kelly Van Nelson. Although deeply serious in tone, this is a creative and theatrical collection that will draw in both fans of the poetry field and new readers to this emotive form of writing. It is clear Kelly Van Nelson is quite the figurehead in terms of contemporary Australian poetry. Her writing is powerful, moody, targeted and emotive. Every word has been carefully selected and each separate poem thoughtfully produced. In this world of increasing domestic violence, continual images of toxic relationship breakdowns, unacceptable attitudes in relation to sexism and negative behaviours, it is high time a progressive collection such as *Punch and Judy* is released in the public sphere. Keynote literature such as *Punch and Judy* can help lead the way in terms of breaking down barriers and can work to change public perceptions with regards to relationship challenges.

Amanda Barrett, Mrs B's Book Reviews

ABANDON SUPERWOMAN

KELLY VAN NELSON

Copyright © Kelly Van Nelson
First published in Australia in 2024
by MMH Press
Waikiki, WA 6169

All Rights Reserved. No part of this book may be used or reproduced by any means, graphic, electronic, or mechanical, including photocopying, recording, taping or by any information storage retrieval system without the written permission of the copyright owner except in the case of brief quotations embodied in critical articles and reviews.

Because of the dynamic nature of the Internet, any web addresses or links contained in this book may have changed since publication and may no longer be vaild. The views expressed in this work are solely those of the author and do not necessarily reflect the views of the publisher and the publisher hereby disclaims any responsibility for them.

 A catalogue record for this work is available from the National Library of Australia

National Library of Australia Catalogue-in-Publication data:
Abandon Superwoman/Kelly Van Nelson

ISBN:
(Paperback)

ISBN:
(eBook)

*For Imani, Holly, Emily,
Elena, Charné and Rebecca
and the next generation of women
taking the world by storm*

LITERARY FICTION

The Pinstripe Prisoner
(Lusaris)
Rolling in the Mud
(Ginninderra Press)

POETRY

Graffiti Lane
(MMH Press)
Punch and Judy
(MMH Press)
Retrospective
(MMH Press)
Graffiti Lane Collector's Edition
(MMH Press)
Globalisation: The Sphere Keeps Spinning
(Compiled by Kelly Van Nelson and MMH Press)

CONTENTS

BLAST OFF 1
A NASA ROCKET TO TEDX 15
CHAPTER AND VERSE 31

    I. LIGHT YEARS 33
    II. MARS 47
    III. VENUS 79
    IV. EARTH 99
    V.. SUN 111
    VI. SATURN 123
    VII. MOON 143
    VIII. KRYPTON 169
    IX. GALAXY 183
    X. MILKY WAY 197

MISSION ACCOMPLISHED 217

BLAST OFF

In the beginning ...

Over 4.5 billion years ago, over the course of seven days, God created the heavens and the earth. He expanded his vision, adding sunlight to make sure we did not all have to face an eternity floundering around in the dark. He also had the foresight to add the Sabbath to ensure we did not go without rest, which was a genius touch given coffee was not invented back then to turbo-boost tired, overworked souls, still searching in vain for better work-life balance.

The biblical story recounts that God fashioned Adam from dust and situated him in the Garden of Eden, telling Adam that he had free reign to feast off every tree in the garden, except for the one tree of the knowledge of good and evil.

Turned out, dinner for one was not too much fun. Subsequently, Eve was created from one of Adam's ribs to serve as his companion. Together, they picked a forbidden *mālum (mālum* is Latin for both apple and evil). Consequently, they were banished into oblivion and at some point bred, and so spawned a new population.

Later, the storytelling prowess of a new literary crowd began to kick in and this talented bunch spread the tale of this gluttonous pair. One of the particularly keen, overachieving authors, rumoured to be named Moses, picked up these rumours second-hand. His creative imagination was fuelled. As such, his pen went to paper, frantically scribbling the ancient chapters of Genesis, depicting in the Bible that women were put on this earth primarily to keep men company.

Yet …

EVOLUTION

Ideas evolve.
Words evolve.
Books evolve.
People evolve.

Long after the Bible became an international bestseller that has so beautifully captured the essence of those early days on earth, DC Comics came along.

Superman was created.

Born on planet Krypton, his parents sent him to earth in a small spaceship just moments before Krypton was destroyed in a natural cataclysm.

Light years later, DC created the concept of Superwoman, a name assigned to several characters in the DC universe who were female versions of Superman.

The first appearance of Superwoman in a DC comic came with Lois Lane dreaming she gained extraordinary powers from a blood transfusion from Superman. The infusion of these incredibly rich male fluids seemingly prompted her to launch a career in journalism.

Who wouldn't be inspired to take after Moses and embark on a career as a writer?

Subsequent stories sporadically featured similar scenarios where Lois gained unique abilities so she could function as a highly capable Superwoman. But in all of these tales, the amazing powers of Superwoman were always temporary, wearing off ahead of those two final words:

The End.

It was not until 2016, when, through *DC Rebirth,* Lois Lane again acquired superpowers, this time not courtesy of any infiltration of foreign male chromosomes into her body, but as the result of a solar energy explosion caused by the death of the New 52 Superman.

Superwoman finally came into her own, becoming the heroine of an ongoing comic book series, with Lois possessing 'all' of Superman's powers.

Woman is no longer man's sidekick. She is a force to be reckoned with in her own right.

Since the beginning of time, through ongoing evolution spanning a period of just a few billion years, women have come a long way. It is finally time to take our rightful place on earth, not just in the home, but in influential positions of political leadership, in the workforce, in the boardroom, in our creative lanes. Wherever we choose to be.

We are no longer the untapped female talent pool of lower-than-male workforce participation. We are finally inhabiting all the spaces we were always meant to occupy, and we are doing so with an abundance of confidence and capability.

For some time now, I have been influencing positive change for women in the workplace, including through submitting positioning papers to government on increasing female apprenticeships and creating safer conditions and improved infrastructure for women in the workplace. Some of these submissions made on behalf of industry were used to shape the new Australian Skills Guarantee that materialised from the 2021 Labor Government Job Summit. Others morphed into keynote speeches to motivate women in leadership or to frame sessions I conducted in schools and universities helping girls and young adults to find ways to overcome obstacles, build capability and establish career pathways best suited to them. I'm proud to have been the winner of various awards surrounding this work, including the Australian AusMumpreneur Awards, the Global Women Changing the World Awards and the Telstra Businesswomen of the Year Awards.

In 2022, *Women's Network Australia* magazine published several of my articles on female empowerment, women's workplace participation in traditionally male-dominated jobs and industries, and owning our own space.

This quote of mine made headlines in an article published in the *Women's Network Australia* magazine:

OUR WORLD

It was never a man's world.
It was always our world too.

I encourage the avoidance of passively waiting for destiny to descend upon you. In sitting with your feet up, sipping the newly invented cappuccino while hoping the stars might one day align. Or blowing out this year's birthday candle and wishing for fate to bring the good fortune of a lucky break.

Instead, consider recognising that the ability to forge our own path lies deep within us all.

In the beginning, Genesis and DC comics chronicled the evolution of women. Today, more than ever before, women are using our powers, intuition and capability to overcome barriers and to make our own decisions.

We are fearlessly carving our own successes and wholeheartedly seeking happiness and fulfilment through conscious choice. It is this exciting journey into the future we must intentionally shape and embrace, for the road leading to this monumental moment of independence has been bumpy at best, treacherous at worst.

With this haiku, I am jumping in the driver's seat to pay it forward, hoping to bring others along for the ride who might need a turbo boost.

TREND-SETTER

*Front foot on the gas,
paying forward, never back,
reversing the trend.*

The concept of this book began with a desire to capture the essence of being a woman. An accolade to the last few years spent living in a parallel universe where writing, business, motherhood and marriage have coexisted, not always in synchronised, harmonious bliss, but intricately intertwined. Instead of loose strands and individual threads, they are weaved into one strong rope, tightly bound together with authenticity.

- *Abandon Superwoman* began as a poem.
- Morphed into a TEDx talk.
- Extended into a manuscript.
- Became my mantra.

I have chosen to no longer be lost in space or to be held captive by the dizziness of a spinning world of competing priorities. Instead, I can be found paused in this single moment in time, captured forever, right here, present on these pages. My hope is that you too might discover a new, unexplored piece of yourself as you read on and that you will be brave enough to take bold new steps to embark along an untrodden path.

The universe can swallow you whole, or you can aim for the stars and land on the moon. Sometimes we just have to fuel up the rocket tank and go for it.

Kelly

xxx

A NASA ROCKET
TO TEDX

A NASA ROCKET TO TEDX

This transcript, titled, *Abandon Superwoman on Krypton,* was a talk delivered in poetic verse by
Kelly Van Nelson.

Amidst the height of the COVID-19 pandemic, due to a period of extended lockdown and strict border closures in Australia, the talk moved suddenly from a scheduled live TEDx event onstage to being virtually streamed live on the TEDx platform. Life can be unpredictable.

It was aired by TEDx on 14 August 2021.
Organised by TEDx Derry Londonderry Studio.
Abandon Superwoman on Krypton
TEDx Talk
was sponsored by:

Poetica
MMH Press
Story Room
WA Poets Inc
Suits or Shirts
Generation Women
Society of Women's Writers NSW
With thanks.

ABANDON SUPERWOMAN ON KRYPTON

I.
A few light years ago
I was working sixteen hours a day
in the corporate world.
At night I was moonlighting as a closet writer,
penning poetry about social issues
into the witching hour,
yet I was intentionally keeping this side of me secret
because I didn't want to be judged for having
this weirdly creative, activist side
of a woman fighting for what I believed was right.
I was also raising two children
and struggling to meet
the simplest family commitment.
My time was compartmentalised
into multiple parallel lives,
but none of them intertwined.
Having these different personas,
each one residing on its own planet,
was hopelessly inefficient
and beyond exhausting.
I was floating around the solar system
with no magnetic pull back
to my true self.
I was trying to be Superwoman
but failing to fly.
I'm Kelly Van Nelson,
executive, poet and mum.

II.
*I grew up in a deprived area
in Newcastle upon Tyne.
It was tough on that rough-cast housing estate,
trying to avoid the inevitable berate
within the woodchipped four walls
of neglect and hate.
Papa died suddenly when his heart
began bleeding instead of beating.
Mama married
again …
and again …
and again …
and we are now estranged,
because even though they say
blood is thicker than water
it can also clot the veins
and I needed to cut the reins
from negativity brain drain
to survive and thrive.
I hoped escape might be at school
but I suffered more than my fair share
of bullying there
for being the dinner ticket kid
trying to blend in
while the hole in my shoe gave me away.
Every day, I wanted to lie down and cry,
it was a do or die situation,
so I left the classroom at sweet sixteen,
waving goodbye to the celestial 'Angel of the North'*

as I travelled on a one-way bus south.
I put myself through night school
to show the world I was no fool
and even though the Queen's English evaded thee
and privilege passed over me
I was damn smart,
playing the part,
refining my art,
giving myself a kick-start,
following premeditated flow chart
into a job
answering the phone,
faxing memo,
trying to erase the memories
of neglected younger years
and all the deeply rooted fears
that I was never going to be good enough
and imposter syndrome would forever be
my only companion.
I developed steely willpower
because nobody who comes from a broken home
wants to be broken
and the bullying that once shattered me
into a million pieces
is now what makes me razor sharp.
All alone in the big smoke,
I learned how to choke back failure,
defeat became alien to me,
reaching my full potential a self-proclaimed prophecy,
the pursuit of success my destiny.

In those troubled years,
where everything was red
and the thin atmosphere was dead,
I learned that the power is mine to reclaim,
just as it is yours —
This is my MARS.

III.
I formed my own family
after finding love in South Africa
with a happily ever after.
Never complacent in the relationship
from the moment it was consummated.
Always refuelling with enough
dangerous heat to melt lead.
Packed every interaction
with action and molten passion.
Radiated lust and tried not
to combust too often,
which seems to have worked.
We are about to celebrate our
silver wedding anniversary —
This is my VENUS.
I won't add URANUS after VENUS
just to show wordsmith genius
or the tone will plummet
with the might of a meteorite
in earthbound flight,
so let's move on.

IV.
We had a daughter,
raised her to be respectful,
but I was neglectful,
it's regretful
that I was the mum who forgot
the oranges at netball,
and who had to buy the cake
for the bake day
because I was so busy trying to pick up
after play date
I forgot to put the tray in the oven on time.
Any working mums out there
resonate with this one?
Dropping the ball
from the moment she forgot to bawl,
started to crawl,
began to fall
into line at school.
I was so busy pinning lists to the fridge
to bridge my own disorganised chaos
I couldn't stop spinning on the axis long enough
to stop the motion sickness,
yet her unconditional love
has always been filled with forgiveness
at my shortfalls
as I tried …
and tried …
and tried …
to make sure she didn't live on MARS

like I once did –
This is my EARTH.

V.
We have a boy too,
a film-making genius who turns my literary word
into a flick that does the trick
of taking my hard-hitting messages
to an audience I want to influence
into changing the world for the better.
Together, he and I think not outside the box,
but like there is no box
as we look past blue sky
to infinity and beyond.
He puts lights, camera, action
on my poetic verse
trying to reverse
the next generation of the underdog
to instil resilience and brilliance
in the lost children
seeking a working-class revolution.
I'm proud of him
for making me look at life through
the next-gen millennium lens
of a person trying to shine the light
on the plight of humanity –
This is my SUN.

VI.
Then there's the pinstripe age
when I'm out of family range
driving organisational change
years after paving the way
from unionised pay
to make hay
at the top of the corporate ladder.
The girl from the street
who wanted to beat
the odds stacked against her.
Combatting perpetuating
education elitism
with determination and realism
in my vocation.
I broke every rule
when I became a mule
smuggling underage innocence
and any lack of brilliance
beneath feigned self-confidence.
Always running rings around the competition
on a mission to be
the best version of me
and helping others to be free
in their thinking.
This ring of ambitious fire
is my passion –
This is my SATURN.

VII.

Then the darkness sets in
and the side hustle kicks in,
as I morph into a poet
with deeply rooted scars
engrained in a sonnet,
sharing verse overflowing
with what's real,
helping to heal
this soul who broke
and was put back together on an open mic
bring every crack in the spotlight,
not caring if this poem is filled
with so many loose threads
it can never be wound on a spool,
because I'm still the goddamn sharpest tool
in the box that you can't box me into,
because I'll always be the girl
who broke every rule in the school
who grew into a woman
who would rather rhyme to make a dime
than decline and recline
back into old skool.
So here I am ...
hands shaking ...
facade breaking ...
these words of truth leaving my tonsils raw
and my heart thumping
on the floor,
exhausted from this stanza bonanza,

*my face beaming with adrenaline
as I cut through the darkness
with the neon starkness of truth –
This is my MOON.
And please, no need to swoon
that I'm the first woman to land on the moon
as I certainly won't be the last.*

VIII.
Eventually, an eclipse came,
causing a collision of parallel lives
in an unsustainable landslide
as I tried to hide behind
a superhero's mask sewn with pride,
instead, crash-landing on unfamiliar territory
barren of fellow human race,
no longer protected by a Kevlar cape
keeping my psyche safe
from the Kryptonite bullets
fired at the escape route
back to my true self.
How many of us are trying
to conform to the norm,
aiming to reform
to take the world by storm,
attempting to transform
into the clone society wants us to become?
In the process of acquiring
the skills required of a senior executive,
building up agility and capability
around strategy and risk and behavioural disc
a crater had formed in my integrity.
It was time to abort being a pocket rocket,
packing in my luggage of courage
into a NASA rocket
launching into space to a place
where I could tenaciously embrace
my flaws,

*because I'm not,
never have been,
never will be,
never want to be
Superwoman.
It's time to leave that side
of the mind behind
with the Kryptonite –
This is my KRYPTON.*

IX.
So here I am …
feet firmly back on the ground,
renewed energy abound,
parallel worlds stranded,
finally landed
right here, right now,
without compartmentalism,
ravishing existentialism
as my mechanism to non-conform
as I abandon Superwoman on KRYPTON.
Arms open as I gulp to fill
starved lungs with oxygen
and authenticity.
Cracks shared,
vulnerability bared,
laser vision no longer impaired
as I realise it's not necessary
to feel the need
to feed and breed duplicity.
I am the dark side of the moon,
the bright side of the sun,
the sparkle of the stars,
with the universe at one –
This is my GALAXY.

X.
Now I'm Kelly Van Nelson,
No longer the exhausted
executive, poet and mum.
I'm just me,
filled with the brightest reality
in a galaxy with no more complexity,
only simplicity and efficiency
in this eighth and final life.
And I want to stay another day,
ignoring the naysayers who say
this MILKY WAY
is just a stepping stone to pave the way
to my ninth and final life,
as whist this might indeed be my plight
it's something I'll fight
because I'm not quite ready
to board that goodnight flight
to my resting place
beside Papa in the afterlife.

TED.COM

ted.com/talks/elly_van_nelson_abandon_superwoman_on_krypton

CHAPTER AND VERSE

I
LIGHT YEARS

A few light years ago I was working sixteen hours a day in the corporate world. At night I was moonlighting as a closet writer, penning poetry about social issues into the witching hour, yet I was intentionally keeping this side of me secret from my network because I didn't want to be judged for having this weirdly creative activist side of a woman fighting for what I believed was right. I was also raising two children and struggling to meet the simplest family commitment. My time was compartmentalised into multiple parallel lives but none of them intertwined. Having different personas, each one residing on its own planet, was hopelessly inefficient and beyond exhausting. I was floating around the solar system with no magnetic pull back to my core true self. I was trying to be superwoman but failing to fly.

I'm Kelly Van Nelson: Executive, poet and mum.

I was thirteen years old when I started work, assuming adult responsibilities to put food on the table. Much of my weekly minimum wage was confiscated by my mother to run the household, so I worked harder, becoming a workaholic while I was still a schoolgirl. As well as earning my keep, going to work was also a way to escape the house and the emotional stress that brewed there. I have never begrudged working a single day and have an ethos of applying my absolute best to whatever I take on.

Over the years, I've built up well-rounded capability, constantly learning and morphing with the times to remain relevant. On many occasions I've been asked to reflect this experience in the form of a summarised biography. I would draft something without ever really thinking about sense of identity. I suspect if I had paused to reflect, I would have found a confused persona who had never received any encouragement before adolescence; an invisible child internalising everything for fear of doing or saying anything that might attract criticism.

As a result, my biography would generally end up as a paragraph or two designed to suit the particular forum in question – a work bio, outlining experience and professional qualifications gained in the corporate world, or an author bio, highlighting writing scholarships and awards, along with literary pieces that had made it into publication. Occasionally, I would be asked about motherhood, so I would tweak the bio again. On review of 'old drafts' of my biography, I can scroll … and scroll … and scroll … through multiple versions, each one individually focused on either work, writing or family.

At some point, well into adulthood, I began to find myself. There was a period of discovering likes and dislikes, jotting them down in expressive, raw poetry. I stopped just going with the flow and figured out the food I really loved, not just what the family like to eat. I perfected my own Spotify musical tastes, tuning in on my kind of beats. And I discovered new countries in the world I had always wanted to explore and found ways to travel to over sixty of them.

Eventually, I had a eureka moment.

Frantically, I scribbled down a biography, not about work, writing or family, but a combination of my whole self, highlighting the fusion of all three.

I tailed it off with the all-encompassing phrase:

I am a juggler.

So many women (and men) I know are juggling home life and family commitments alongside their job, and are then trying to squeeze in their creative passion in whatever spare few nanoseconds they can scrape together.

Compartmentalising is a common technique people adopt to deal with life's competing priorities in a more manageable way. It is a fairly common method to bring order to the chaos of everything being thrown at you.

The more control and focus that one can create in the present moment can 'sometimes' result in not only less stress but improved productivity and more quality time.

For years, this was me. Life was hurtling along, compartmentalised into three parallel worlds, all competing for time, energy and my full attention.

- Work.
- Writing.
- Home.

Before my first book came out, I had hardly told a soul about my secret life as a writer, but as my work made it into various publications, the cat finally clawed its way out of the bag. It has led to one of the most common questions I get asked at author talks:

'How do you juggle everything?'

At first, I found myself dancing around this conundrum. I'd never allowed myself a breather to look at the big picture around the direction life had taken. Yet this frequently posed question played on my mind, challenging me to stop and think about how I was managing so many moving parts.

I realised, in part, that I was only managing to cram everything into these siloed compartments by sustaining excessively long days, which came courtesy of insomnia.

For a long time, insomnia and I had a love-hate relationship. I relished the fact I could get by on less sleep than most, and in general, remain able to function, more often than not with above-average, high outputs. Insomnia, when looking at it with kind eyes, allowed me to have extended late-night hours when I could be seduced by words without interruption. But without rose-tinted goggles, chronic insomnia was the ravishing devil of darkness who never left any corner of the mind unoccupied, relentlessly consuming every second it could in a vice grip of insatiable greed. Sleep was the enemy.

Only in my forties, during the COVID lockdowns, did I decide to have a go at trying to find a more balanced sleep pattern. The reset of the pandemic forced me to recognise that in the long-term, deprivation of decent levels of shut-eye could no doubt lead to health problems. I doubled down on exercise, wearing down my body into tired submission. I began adjusting my alarm clock by fifteen-minute intervals, letting my body adapt to the gradual change for a few weeks at a time. It worked. I've finally managed to move my average sleep per night from what was a meagre four hours to a respectable seven.

Sleep is key for the brain to think clearly and function at optimum levels and to allow the body to recoup and maintain physical health. It takes determination to correct a sleep pattern developed over a lifetime, yet even the most deeply rooted habits can indeed be broken.

Looking back, there was never a conscious decision to embrace insomnia for so long and to compartmentalise my life. It just subconsciously morphed this way over time. It never once dawned on me that the approach I was taking could possibly be a defence mechanism to avoid anxiety and dissonance in everyday life. It was a maladaptive coping strategy that tipped over into being mentally taxing and physically exhausting. Yet, in hindsight, I can now see living this way, hurtling along from one task to the next, sleeping minimal hours, trying to be perfect, juggling multiple competing priorities while frequently dropping the ball, was emotionally suppressive and stressful.

We do not have to neglect ourselves or put our own wellbeing second because we are so busy being everything to everyone else that we have stretched ourselves to breaking point. No more juggling the career, family, home, exercise, social activities, hobbies and passions every minute of every day.

We do not have to suffer from Superwoman syndrome.

All of us deserve a life where we do not constantly feel frazzled by having to manage so many competing priorities. We owe it to ourselves to enjoy downtime and appreciate restful pause. To sleep and allow the body and mind to replenish. To relish in the golden moments of being fully present and fully immersed in whatever life is presenting in the here and now.

To live one holistic life.

STARGAZER MOMENT

*Seek
to replenish sleep,
banking it to keep
replenished.*

- Exercise regularly during the day, finishing physical activity at least three hours before bed to allow your body to wind down.
- Keep both mind, as much as the body, active in the day, resulting in physical and mental wellness, resting both adequately at night to replenish the batteries.
- Try to form a habit of waking at the same time each day, even if it is tempting to snooze late on weekends or take daytime naps.
- Adapt your sleep patterns over time, with the use of an alarm clock, making careful adjustments, until you have trained your body to become accustomed to the desired amount of shut-eye.
- Eliminate the consumption of alcohol and caffeine which may impact your ability to fall asleep or have an initial sedative effect then result in you awakening through the night.
- Avoid drinking excessive fluids before bed which can also prompt an overactive bladder, waking you for frequent bathroom visits so you suffer from broken sleep.
- Avoid eating or snacking too close to bedtime which can kick the digestive system into action.

- Manage stress levels before bed, listing any goals or plans well ahead of turning out the light at the end of the day.
- If your mind is prone to worrying at night, try a bath, reading or deep breathing techniques before going to bed to relax the body and mind.
- Ensure your bed is comfortable and your room ambience is aligned to winding down. Opt for controlled lighting and reduced noise levels if you can, using an eye mask and earplugs if needed.
- Keep the bedroom sacred for sleeping and sex. Avoid watching television or using devices in bed *(sex devices excluded)*.

How can you selfishly ensure you get enough rest to be at your best?

_____

_____

_____

_____

_____

What can you consciously adjust to knock bad habits on the head?

_____

_____

_____

_____

_____

In the face of adversity, how can you be mercenary in replenishing your energy?

_____

_____

_____

_____

II
MARS

I grew up in a deprived area of Newcastle upon Tyne. It was tough on that rough-cast council estate, trying to avoid the inevitable berate within the wood-chipped four walls of neglect and hate. Papa died suddenly in his forties when his heart began bleeding instead of beating. Mama married again and again and again, and we are now estranged, because even though they say blood is thicker than water, it can also clot the veins and I needed to cut the reigns from negativity brain drain to survive and thrive.

I hoped escape might be at school, but I suffered more than my fair share of bullying there for being the dinner ticket kid trying to blend in while the hole in my shoe gave me away. Every day I wanted to lie down and cry, it was a do or die situation, so I left the classroom at sweet sixteen, waving goodbye to the celestial Angel of the North as I travelled on a one-way bus south.

I put myself through night school to show the world I was no fool even though the Queen's English evaded thee and privilege passed over me, I was damn smart, playing the part, refining my art, giving myself a kickstart, following premeditated flow chart into a job, answering the phone, faxing memo, trying to erase the memories of neglected younger years and all the deeply rooted fears that I was never going to be good enough and imposter syndrome would forever be my only companion.

I developed steely willpower because nobody who comes from a broken home wants to be broken and the bullying that once shattered me into a million pieces is now what makes me razor sharp.

All alone in the big smoke I learned how to choke back failure. Defeat became alien to me. Reaching my full potential a self-proclaimed prophecy. The pursuit of success my destiny. In those troubled years, where everything was red and the thin atmosphere was dead, I realised the power is mine to reclaim, just as it is yours.

This is my Mars.

Growing up was tough. I was an underprivileged kid blending in with the rough-cast, grey, pebble stones of the council estate walls in Newcastle upon Tyne. A rebel without a cause, hanging tough behind the graffitied dustbins at the back of the grocery store. The consumer of ten pence cigarettes and a bottle of Scrumpy Jack passed around desolate teenagers sharing a survival mission together.

It's a fair statement to say my childhood was as far removed from a silver spoon upbringing as one can get. The kind where every surface was made of concrete and there was no safety net at the park. In fact, there was not only no safety net – there was no park.

My parents were sixteen, still in high school when they got married. My mother had my sister at seventeen, me at nineteen, divorced my father not long after, then remarried. In my youngest childhood years, I lived with her Monday to Friday, spending weekends with my father. I recall Friday nights when he came to collect me and my older sister. World War III would take place on the front lawn as my mother launched surface-to-air missiles at him.

Memories of growing up are filled with angst, dogged by recollections of household arguments bursting through the walls with an intense ferocity that had me cowering under the covers in bed. I would read endless Enid Blyton books by torchlight, escaping reality in the tales of *Malory Towers* and lands of *The Faraway Tree*. I would carve reading time into the early hours of the morning, spent with a good book, devoured under the duvet by torchlight.

My body adapted to operating with extremely low levels of sleep, with the acute insomnia of adulthood developing as a young child. This nightly practice of escaping reality within the words of a good book was a protection mechanism against the many fights, verbal and physical, that went on in our household. I developed an uncanny ability to filter out a substantial amount of noise. This is a skill that has served me well over the years as I have two children who both play musical instruments – one the piano, the other the electric guitar. I was still in high school when my older sister left home and I become the sole occupant of our bunkbeds in our previously shared bedroom. I began swapping this bedtime ritual of reading with using the late-night window to put pen to paper, producing much of my earliest literary work in the dead of the night.

While home life was tough, unfortunately school was no better. Not long into my teenage years we moved to a new house, across the Tyne River to the other side of town, which also meant moving high schools. I was the new girl on the block in a public school where I didn't know a soul. For the lion's share of my high school years, I was bullied. Never physically, but verbal abuse in the corridor was a daily occurrence. I became a verbal punching bag for the mean girls at school.

STICKS AND STONES

*Verbal sticks and
demeaning stones
tossed my way
can't break my bones
instead they crush
sensitive soul
into the pavement
t'was mean-girl's goal
stomped between cracks
chewed up gum
nothing more than
a nuisance —
you done?*

School corridors were brutal. Attempts to become invisible by hunching my shoulders to make myself smaller and dropping my head to avoid eye contact failed to divert my back being a target. I tried to cut off thinking about being verbally abused after the 3pm bell went, compartmentalising school into its box and tuning it out however I could, usually with the help of drink and recreational drugs consumed with the friends I did have. I used the antidotes of reading and writing when I was in solitude.

Home, school and spare time were completely separate environments running in parallel to one another. None but two of my closest school friends and my sister know just how big a mess my life was back then.

Yet those early years shaped some lifelong habits.

I found the yin in my love for reading, which morphed into a love for writing. In the darkness of night, I escaped reality when I shone that torch beam onto the infinite possibilities of imagination.

In the face of adversity, I chose to carve a different path. To not accept the status quo and to buck against the foregone conclusion of becoming a product of my environment. Many things were out of my control, but I recognised I still had the ability to make certain choices.

At the age of thirteen, I began working part-time outside of school hours, in a hairdressers, then a bakery and for a short while flipping burgers. I knew I wanted to become self-sufficient, which in my mind was a simple as wanting to be able to move out of the house.

I had visions of being an au pair, working on a cruise ship or joining the crew for an airline, any of which would take me as far away from home as possible. I quite seriously contemplated joining the army, and in fact did my work experience at Catterick Garrison in my teens, which I loved. However, there were next to no girls taking this path at the time and I recall my teacher actively discouraging me from joining the military because I was not the right gender for this to be a sound career choice. I still have bitter regrets that I listened to such nonsense and have the utmost respect for the many serving women (and men) in defence who have played a part in allowing diversity to flourish in the workforce and for selflessly putting the safety of others first.

It's one of life's gifts that I've come full circle and am now heavily involved in the defence industry as part of my corporate work. Being involved in protecting our national interests, the freedom we so often take for granted, and the lives of people going about their daily business is beyond rewarding.

Even though I may only be a very small cog in an enormous wheel, I am proud to be contributing in some way to Defence Enterprise. I'm a regular keynote speaker at major Women in Defence events and conferences. These forums can often be quite traditional in format and rigid in agendas, but countless times, I've respectfully broken the mould while still keeping on point and to the session theme at hand. On a few occasions I've incorporated a poem of mine, titled *Uncle Sam,* into my sessions, pointing to that early experience of being a female discouraged from joining the military.

UNCLE SAM

*My teenage body germinating
a coming-of-age mentality,
sat upright the day the troops stormed class
to recruit all the lads; I was the only lass
who raised a voluntary arm
still numb from the BCG vaccine
regime designed to make sure we were a pristine,
clean, human machine
to be taken away to glean our dreams
and carve core skills to make the next generation
of privates who could scale military ranks
from frontline trenches to driving tanks.*

*It was the first time I'd ever seen green
in an otherwise grey world
and I was drawn to the appeal
of stepping into newly camouflaged skin
where I would never be a misfit again;
relishing the idea of modelling a child's uniform
that blended in to be the exactly the same
as every other figure in the frame,
giving adequate protection from the giveaway
of a hole in trainers from the mart
that spelled out the cruel fact
I could never master the art
of looking like a kid born with privilege.*

*The jabbed bruise on my arm screamed
to be selected for work experience,
desperate to punch higher
than the heavy weight of a weary heart
sparring to have a fighting start in life.*

*They marched me away for a training day,
to tackle mud run pain
with the lure of regular pay
and a compass as my new friend
desperately trying to show the way
to a utopian place where north
had all the magnetic pull on the planet
before my teacher rained on the parade,
pointing out I was the only female applicant
who didn't fit the profile of a regular candidate,
leaving my aspirations wounded …
unable to soldier on.*

*Taking a bullet isn't fatal
when resilience is made from Kevlar
built up over years of living in the conflict zone
of a broken home
in an inner city prone
to never throwing the dog a bone.*

*I soldiered on, taking a new tact
of building a career down another track
onto the battlefield we all must combat
to infiltrate the employment field.*

*Over time the rules of engagement changed
with women beginning to make the grade,
lining up after graduation convocation
to gain the accolade of fighting
for their country
in the search
for equality.*

*These nieces of Uncle Sam
are in the army now,
even though I
am not.*

*Instead, I wave my flag at full mast
because the battle of these women
making it in a historical man's world
is won.*

Back then, that same teacher who discouraged me enlisting, convinced me that getting an entry-level job in an office would be the best possible way to use my brains to generate a steady income. At the time, this appealed, as this option resonated in my mind with achieving financial independence, which I thought could still give me a 'way out' of life at home.

Aside from harbouring a goal of earning my own keep any way I could to become self-sufficient, the one consistent dream that was all-consuming was that I wanted to write.

Whenever I had spare time, I would mess around writing poems or song lyrics and was an attentive student of English literature, taught by a teacher who loved the classics. I listened and learned about Shakespeare, Wilde and Hemmingway, but my passions were secretly in the immediate beauty of the modern day and the ordinary. The starkness of a fluorescent light. Spray paint on a brick wall. Gum in the cracks on the pavement. They signalled the underbelly of life.

Classic or contemporary, a love of reading and writing was part of my daily ritual. A way to unwind after a long, unhappy day at school or work. To switch off from reality. To tune out.

My closest school friends recall me citing an ambition when I was around thirteen years old that I was going to write a book one day.

Not once did I ever doubt that I could do it.

I dreamt bigger than my current circumstances and strived for something greater than what was in front of me.

THE PROMISES I KEEP

*Keeping to your word is free,
costing only tenacity
and integrity.*

Back to choice. With youth came the decision of taking a path paved with either delinquency or art. I chose to immerse myself in creativity in the form of reading and writing for self-preservation. Words on the page provided a coping mechanism to shield myself from the volatile jeering and elbows in the school corridors. The older I got, the less power the popular masses had, especially after I finally stood up for myself one day and called the worst school bully out on her behaviour.

Mastering the ability to stand up for yourself and brush yourself off when you are kicked down is a lifelong skill worth developing.

ROOMMATES

*I am not my environment
and my environment is not me –
We are only ever just roommates for a while.*

Overcoming a turbulent childhood is what lies at the core of my DNA. If a scientist were to swab under my Geordie native tongue, no doubt the results would show genes of resilience that have mutated over the years to reframe the bittersweet taste of life's truths into something people like to call a 'thick skin'.

Somewhere in my late teens, I realised I wanted more than what the naked eye can see on the horizon. I had no clue what the 'more' was. Only that I didn't want to face the sunset each day having only ever lived amongst the shadows of the concrete streets.

I wanted to see a sunrise spread her bright aura across somewhere other than one of the most deprived areas of the UK. A burning desire to explore the unknown began to surface. I wanted to leave the 'toon', stroll down an unknown road, ignore all the signposts and get lost along the way.

My earliest objectives around reshaping the status quo were simple:

- Rewrite the blueprint.
- Break the mould.
- Smash through glass ceilings.

On the outside, peer pressure had some impact, doing its best to condition my appearance to fit in with the homeland crowd. I wore a colourful cheap nylon shell suit and brandless trainers. My fringe was hair-sprayed into classic eighties stiffness. Newcastle United black and white stripes were the bars of my cell; the Saturday afternoon football scarf a noose around my neck ready to hang myself.

I was being conditioned to stay, but all the while I was there, singing Blaydon Races from the St James Park bleachers with the rest of the magpie die-hard fans, *haiku* verse would come to mind.

MAGPIE

*Black and white magpie
flying without flock, lonesome
bird without feather.*

On the inside, I protected my critical organs with a multi-million NASA spacesuit designed of my newly grown thick skin. This offered daily protection from radiation permeating:

- From homelife.
- From school.
- From myself.

At the time, protective hazmat gear available to the general population was not a thing. Nobody had a stockpile of masks to protect from breathing in harmful viral infections. There was little to no protection outside my own defence mechanisms. No school counsellors to go to for a chinwag to relieve steam during break time or to drop in a recurrence block booking of ten sessions of therapy in the iPhone calendar. At the time there were few other options other than to drop your head to the knees, protect the skull with your hands and remain in the assumed brace position until the blows raining down eventually ceased.

Yet there is always choice.

I could determine how to respond to these alien attacks threatening to destabilise my wellbeing. I opted to suffer the onslaught, then recover silently and swiftly. In hindsight, this was my conditioning to 'go it alone', and somehow, I always knew I would be successful on my mission.

- My body became scarred from the wounds of childhood.
- My mind became dark, questioning the meaning of existence.
- My soul became bright, planning for a journey to the unknown.

The vacuum of outer space represents a particularly challenging environment for human exploration, not least because of dealing with the hazard of constant radiation.

Growing up, inside the woodchip-clad walls of our council house, it was brutally cold. Tension bounced around the place, mixed with fragmented arguments. On more than one occasion I was frozen to the spot while being beaten black and blue. On another, my sister picked nits from my head as we shivered together sharing a rare lukewarm bath. We were always filthy, with few clothes and no toiletries. When I look back in search of childhood memories with a glimmer of joy, my only recollections of life at home are of deep sadness and acute fear.

Fear, in its destructive form, can be all-consuming to the point of helplessness. Finding coping methods to avoid complete debilitation from this unwanted invisible force can be what saves you from falling into the traps of depression and anxiety.

There is also no atmosphere in space, which means that sound has no way to travel and so cannot be heard.

I never once screamed.

Even when stinging handprints were imprinted on my body and I was so sore I could not sit down. Fear never paralysed my mind from crossing the harsh terrain from hell to a better mental place in silence.

There are always free resources available in the inner sanctuary of our minds. In the face of adversity, I found a way to access the free tool of 'affirmations'.

- You can escape the radiation.
- You shall pass through the vacuum.
- You will be heard.

I have never and will never profess to be a professional on how to overcome trauma, but I will share one of the pieces of advice most frequently given to me over the years.

Embrace imperfection by using empowering affirmations, supplemented with calming breathing techniques.

I've certainly mastered the use of affirmations over time. There is a simple poem from my poetry book, *Retrospective*. It is a calling to the childhood affirmation that has underground roots from way back growing up in Newcastle upon Tyne.

HEY, TEACHER,

I am good enough.
I am good enough.
I am good enough.
I am good enough.
I am good enough.
I am good enough.
I am good enough.
I am good enough.
I am good enough.
I am good enough.
I am good enough.
I am good enough.
I am good enough.
I am good enough.
I am good enough.
I am good enough.
I am good enough.
I am good enough.

While affirmation has enormous benefits in building self-worth, managing to sustain a steady breathing pattern while under substantial pressure has proven much more difficult an art for me to master.

In the moments where I am not in control of a difficult situation – for example where core values or basic ethics are under attack or profound uncertainty lingers – I get a tightness of the windpipe and a red blush physically rises up my neck as I struggle to breathe. In these moments, I try to think about the given situation and how I want it to transpire and come out the other side. I remind myself you can only guarantee the way you manage yourself, so attempt to do this to the best of your abilities. No matter what you do, you cannot be responsible for the behaviours of everyone else all of the time.

The same goes if I am giving a keynote speech on stage and feel the nerves threaten to take over my vocal cords and freeze my brain. I picture myself delivering my words and content with confidence and conviction, inspiring at least one person attending to take something positive away from the experience, rather than piling on the pressure that I have to win over the whole audience.

For anyone who gets stage fright, try to remind yourself before you freeze up that there is no point worrying about the entire crowd. No two perspectives are the same. We are all unicorns (thank goodness!). There will always be someone out there who sees the world through a different lens. Some will adopt a steely, critical glare, others will wear rose-tinted glasses.

Instead of trying to please everyone, latch on to the idea that there will likely be at least one person in the crowd listening, searching for inspiration, hoping for a revelation. So instead of trying to change the world, evolve aspirations to simply wanting to improve it, positively influencing one person at a time.

A business coach once told me that everyone has a superpower and that mine is the extraordinary amount of positive energy which flows through my body. She worked with me to find ways to ground and bottle this fizzing energy. To be more centred on my axis. Otherwise, I run the risk of spinning to the point of sickness and frazzling myself and others. I take this as a compliment for this superpower allows me to achieve the impossible.

***Impossible
or
I'm
Possible.***

If you feel a similar energy rush before presenting, or have a tidal wave of nerves in the middle of a tricky conversation, or have anxiety relative to a particular situation that threatens to choke the throat, you can let the nerves kick in and passively allow your voice to get the shakes – or you can pause to regroup.

Take a moment to apply a short-term fix technique, silently replay your affirmation. Allow yourself the luxury of a few moments to steady the breath, calm the mind and focus the fizzing energy.

Someone in the audience needs you.

This simple technique works well for me in the short-term gain. However, breathing and affirmation has just not been enough for me to entirely move past the fear in the long-term.

I left school at sixteen, not because I was not smart enough to further my education, but because the vacuum of life threatened to swallow me whole and the radiation was poisonous. So, I booked a one-way ticket to London, not on a NASA rocket, but on the National Express bus to adulthood. There was no fear, only fizzing energy.

There were not too many coins rattling in my pocket, but I had my resources:

- Pen.
- Paper.
- Ambition.

The literary word in the form of reading and writing provided a vehicle to escape reality whenever I needed it, providing a means to be transported to somewhere else. Somewhere infinitely better. Words revived my dead batteries with a much-needed invisible energy boost. They provided a way to avoid dwelling on what was a lousy home and school life. While I craved normal parents and a quiet window at school, there was little to be gained from letting the lack of such luxuries throw me into oblivion.

I refused to allow myself to remain a resident on the cold desert planet that was Mars, aptly named after the Roman god of war. The only solution was to escape. To release myself from the past and to try to become a better person than the parenting I received.

POWERHOUSE

*We have the power
of choice; to reclaim a life
of our own design.*

Those early days shaped who I am and led to the very different family dynamics I sought out for myself as an adult.

- A kind, unselfish husband who always puts others first.
- Children who I love with every inch of my soul.
- A home filled with warmth and joy.

This childhood DNA is the root cause of every crack in the armour, yet it is also the glue keeping my toughened character from falling apart.

STARGAZER MOMENT

*No procrastination
in the application
of affirmation.*

- Place both hands on your stomach to consciously focus on breath and energy.
- Mentally repeat your chosen affirmation phrase three times:
  - I am cool.
  - I am calm.
  - I am centred.
- Breathe in through the nose for 4 seconds.
- Hold your breath for 4 seconds.
- Exhale through the mouth for 4 seconds.
- Hold your breath for 4 seconds.
- Repeat this process three times.

What affirmation phrase will shift your psyche to a more positive frame?

_____

_____

_____

_____

What is your superpower?

_____

_____

_____

_____

_____

How can you use your superpower to influence your own mindset and that of others?

_____

_____

_____

_____

_____

III
VENUS

I formed my own family after finding love in South Africa with a happily ever after, never complacent in the relationship from the moment it was consummated, always ensuring it was refuelled with enough dangerous heat to melt lead. Made sure every interaction was packed with action and molten passion. Radiated lust and tried not to combust too often. It seems to have worked. We are about to celebrate our silver wedding anniversary.

This is my Venus.

(I won't add Uranus after Venus just to show wordsmith genius, or the tone will plummet with the might of a meteorite in earthbound flight, so let's move on).

It was the eve of my nineteenth birthday when I first met my husband-to-be, and we are still together today. I like to think our relationship has lasted this long not because *men are from Mars and women are from Venus,* but because we both reside together on Venus … at least some of the time.

Venus is the brightest planet in the solar system and is hot enough to melt lead. Also a Roman goddess, Venus has the encompassing traits of love, beauty, desire, sex, fertility, prosperity and victory.

What is not to like about a place like this?

Although it pains me to admit it, something this fiery has downsides. At some point it seems Venus transformed from being a potentially habitable world to its current hellish state where nothing can survive. This serves as a cautionary tale on how dramatically positive dynamics can shift. You therefore have to work at marriage, so it does not ever become inhabitable.

It can be difficult balancing love and career. My husband and I both work in full-time employment. As a mum of two, being employed in multinationals for many years at executive level, life has been crazy busy for as long as I can remember. Quality time can very quickly become an unattainable wish. A heightened imbalance between the job and the relationship can be a fatal trap to fall into.

Venus can very quickly become hostile.

We have managed to overcome work pressures in our own way, which is not to say these methods will work for everyone else. Every relationship has its own unique characteristics, and I am certainly not professing to be a marriage counsellor. But there are ways we have avoided Venus becoming a barren desert.

TROUBLE AND STRIFE

*Never sacrifice
what's most important in life
or end up in strife.*

Living on Venus as a career-oriented couple with kids can be 'full on'. It needs careful balance, so the most important stuff still happens.

Early in our relationship, we tackled the way we would manage finances. Money has never really become a point of tension, even when we have been broke.

We have found a way to share the household chores through allowing each other to gravitate to the ones we each naturally prefer.

When we do have a blow up, we try not to carry a grudge over to the next day.

And we hold on tightly to the boundaries we want to keep firmly in place. These can be anything from firmly declining late Friday night virtual work meetings, ensuring one of us always attends any major events of importance to the kids or keeping Sundays free and easy, unofficially reserved for quality family time and a cocktail or two.

WEATHER THE STORM

*Take risks together
and learn to weather
the storm.*

Over the last three decades, my husband and I have lived on the bread line in a bedsit in Kings Cross, London, built up a decent nest egg, lost it all during the GFC, opened a restaurant and closed it, built up another nest egg, and lived in over twenty houses spanning three continents.

We have embraced new ideas, taken untested roads, and never looked at major moves as a crazy idea fraught with danger.

Over a glass of wine, we have considered each opportunity that has presented itself and decided to grab it with both hands. We look at each situation with open eyes and generally reach a mutual understanding of the calculated risks we are taking on. At times we have carved out our own new experiences, as a way to evolve and build upon the past we have already had. Each time we face something new, we have weighed up the worst case. When we look at 'what if', we generally land on the answer that life would still go on.

We might quit our jobs, leave behind friends, sell up a home we have lovingly renovated, but when it comes down to it, we can find another gig with enhanced career prospects, form new friendship circles and accessorise a new pad.

Positive risk-taking keeps things interesting, enabling us to individually stretch ourselves while allowing our family to become more resilient and grow together.

Taking major decisions as one family unit has helped us be more independent, confident, braver and stronger, in pursuing the life of our choosing.

In facing the possibility of failure and overcoming fears to advance into unexplored terrain, try to take pause.

Instead of the different options rendering you overwhelmed with confusion, look at the positives of stepping out of your comfort zone and let the excitement of pushing the boundaries take up some space.

- Walls can be climbed.
- Glass ceilings are there to be broken.
- Dreams can be made a reality.

If you do find yourself in difficult territory, trenches can be manufactured if you are prepared to dig deep, go the hard yards and get on with tackling whatever the issue is as a team.

As a result of taking chances, you may just benefit from so many new and enriching experiences that you will create a life of no regrets.

WEAR AND TEAR

*Surviving
wear and tear
when I am here
and you are there
is easy to bear
by reviving
self-care.*

Many couples have the luxury of seeing each other every day. That is not the case for us. I travel extensively as part of my corporate role, sometimes for months on end. Just to add to the hectic lifestyle, my husband has also spent extensive periods of time away from home doing work requiring him to fly in and out of remote locations. Sometimes neither of us are on Mars or Venus at all. We are at opposite ends of the solar system on foreign planets.

During COVID, my husband was working in Western Australia while I was on the East Coast working in lockdown conditions and looking after the kids who had to homeschool for months on end. Stringent border restrictions between the Australian states and territories meant he went from Flying In Flying Out (FIFO) fortnightly to going several months at a time before we could see each other. My husband was subjected to six rounds of fourteen days isolation in order to travel home from work to spend time with the family. Yet we came out of the other side, and for that, I am grateful.

RED DUST

I wore white once,
bronze shoulders, blue garter, gold ring,
strolled the aisle with pride,
you by my side,
bound by our partnership oath.
Honeymoon wanderlust,
credit card bust,
I was me,
you were you,
we were us,
two decades ago,
before red dust.

I was me once,
northern girl with the English fair skin,
you were you once,
African boy, our souls were akin,
we were us once,
no money, but inseparable.
Carved a life on a dime,
I learned how to rhyme,
entry ticket into the land of red dust.
Now I free flow while you FIFO,
but I'm still me,
you're still you,
we're still us.

When the beat in life changes,
it fucks you up,
roll with it, suck it up.
High viz, steel caps, two weeks on,
barbeque, jujitsu, two weeks off,
red dust, no us, two weeks on,
red lipstick, date night, two weeks off,
red dust, two weeks on,
red lipstick, two weeks off,
red dust, red lipstick,
red dust, red lipstick,
two weeks on, two weeks off,
two weeks on, two weeks off,
I'm still me,
you're still you,
we're still us,
red dust.

You flew out, two weeks on, that was then,
before COVID pandemic claimed our men,
and women and them,
the old, vulnerable.
Now our airlines are bust
and you're beached in red dust;
I'm alone behind mask to protect
viral particles taking hostage of breath,
borders closed with me east while you're in the west,
different time, different place, watch sunset —
marriage test.

We call and we zoom and facetime,
Whatsapp, RUOK, I ask you.
Ek kan nie nou praat nie, you tell me.
I can't speak at the moment, ok.
Whatsapp, RUOK, Whatsapp, RUOK,
ek kan nie nou praat nie, RUOK?

I'm still me, I'm still here,
you're still you, you're still there,
we're still us, on the east and the west.
Fifty weeks, not two weeks, was the on,
permission slip to make a trip home,
red lipstick back on, all dressed up,
barbecue, Jujitsu, two weeks off.

Each day a reborn honeymoon,
skin to skin not on Facetime or Zoom,
but too soon you've to pack,
quarantine or the sack,
me and kids on end of the phone, you alone.
ISO / SOS / ISO / SOS / ISO / SOS /
RUOK?

We do what we do
and we love over Zoom,
I'm still me, I'm still here,
you're still you, you're still there,
we're still us on the east and the west,
red dust.

FIFO, ek kan nie nou praat nie.
ISO, ek kan nie nou praat nie.
FIFO / RUOK / ISO / RUOK /
FIFO, ek kan nie nou praat nie.

When dust settles the red tape gets cut,
I'm still me, you're still you, we're still us.
We're red dust / SOS /
we're red dust / SOS /
we're red dust, not ok –
SOS.

(Translation Afrikaans to English: Ek kan nie nou praat nie = I can't talk now).

Being in a long-distance relationship, if left to trundle along, could bring difficulties to any partnership. For us, we have positively faced into it, applying practicalities that help continuity of the day-to-day trifles while also protecting the sacred cow of quality time when we are together.

Picking up the phone, placing a video call each day and messaging regularly, has worked for us to ensure we look out for each other no matter where we are based. We communicate constantly, even when we are miles apart. Technology has become our best friend in making sure the trivial things as well as anything on the big-ticket horizon get discussed and we remain connected.

We plan holidays together whenever we can, alternate visits to see each other, meeting in places away from home that are convenient to wherever one of us is working so we build anticipation and have something to look forward to. But we also embrace spur-of-the-moment decision-making, going out for dinner if we feel like it or grabbing a night away 'just because'. We never plan 'date nights'. Instead, we prioritise spontaneous 'dating' as part of the way we coexist to keep the Roman goddess spark alive.

STARGAZER MOMENT

*I won't waste my breath on someone
who isn't able to take my breath away;
leave me breathless
or leave me.*

- Communicate frequently, even when apart.
- Keep boundaries and the important things sacred.
- Live in the moment, grab spontaneous date nights and generate new experiences on the spur of the moment.
- Create equity in managing finances, household decision-making and the pursuit of careers.
- Don't try to rotate chores evenly; play to each other's natural preferences and skills.
- Live on the edge once in a while. Take some chances together, weighing up the pros and cons to develop a mechanism to assess opportunities and get comfortable with the risk.
- Think about the upside of change to move past the fear of failure.
- Remember Venus can very quickly become inhospitable if you don't respect the terrain.

How can you improve communications to reduce tension with your partner?

_____

_____

_____

_____

What new experiences can you introduce to produce a fresh spark in your relationship?

_____

_____

_____

_____

What calculated risk will help you persist in pursuing a life with no regrets?

_____

_____

_____

_____

_____

IV
EARTH

We have a daughter. Raised her to be respectful, but I was neglectful, it's regretful that I was the mum who forgot the oranges at netball, and who had to buy the cake for the bake day because I was so busy picking up after play dates I forgot to put the tray in the oven on time.

Any working mums out there resonate with this one?

Dropping the ball from the moment the youngest forgot to bawl, started to crawl, began to fall into line at school. I was so busy trying to pin lists to the fridge to bridge my own disorganised chaos I couldn't stop spinning on the axis long enough to stop the motion sickness, yet her unconditional love has always been filled with forgiveness at my shortfalls as I tried and tried and tried to make sure she didn't live on Mars like I once did.

This is my earth.

The day my daughter was born brought me down to earth with a bang. Here she was, unassuming, innocent and wholly dependent.

Earth is the only astronomical object known to harbour life and Mother Earth is a common personification of the giver and sustainer of life. I had brought another human being into this world, and I wanted to forever be the best Mother Earth to this beautiful baby girl.

As a mum, I very quickly learned how to do multiple things at once. I could feed my newborn while making a phone call. Prepare dinner for my husband while carrying my bub on my back. Send an important email while tapping the baby bouncer with my foot. While my husband was out at work, I learned to be the queen of multitasking. While at home on maternity leave, I would be the time-efficient juggler of multiple balls. I would be Super Mum.

I did not want my daughter to crave maternal love or want for anything like I had to as a child. There was an invisible pressure of sorts to be the perfect parent. There were also many other opinions to consider. Those of the midwife on whether to breastfeed or not. Advice from family members and friends who had their own children and ideals around how to raise a baby. Daytime TV programs on how to nurture a healthy family. Adverts on which diapers to choose. I didn't want to be shamed for doing the wrong thing, or even worse, made to feel ashamed for not doing something at all. So, I juggled some more.

Yet inevitably, I would make a mistake. I would toss up all the balls and one of them would crash to the floor.

At the time it never occurred to me that dropping the ball is actually a positive. By default, it means we have one less thing to juggle and can therefore put extra effort onto the others still in the air.

Nobody told me to count every single ball I was managing to

keep up and to give myself some credit for it. This was the advice I would have welcomed, rather than let it fester in my mind that I was inadequate because one had inadvertently slipped through my hands.

Hindsight is a wonderful thing.

When I look back, I cringe at the moment when it was my turn to take the oranges to netball for half-time nutrition and I clean forgot. Instead, I gave the girls a couple of jelly snakes each, and albeit this was not my finest moment aligned to healthy eating, the sugar fix seemed to give them the boost of energy needed to make it to the final whistle. They won the match.

I still break out into a cold sweat when I think about time I got the date wrong for one of my daughter's friend's birthday parties and we were stuck without a gift, yet we improvised and the workaround was just fine.

Parenting isn't about being perfect, attending every school invite, cramming in the never-ending stream of extracurricular activities or becoming president of the PTA. It's an impossible standard to keep and can also send the wrong message to our children just as much as not attending anything at all would have a negative impact.

There is a balance in everything. Rather than spreading precious time too thin, a better outcome can be found from more selectively choosing where to put quality time and energy, then giving it your all.

There are so many incredible mothers out there who hustle like crazy all day long, beating themselves up for not managing to contribute to the school bake sale or for not coping with the competing pressures of a work deadline that falls on the same day as the school swim carnival.

We've all done it. Struggled to keep up the shopfront and avoided asking others for help. At the same time, we internalise the reality of any form of unwanted chaos. We feel broken if something 'has to give' instead of rejoicing in the transience of our beautifully flawed lives.

At one point in time or another, we are all going to drop the ball. It is a fact that no matter how hard we try to do it all, and do it all well, we will inevitably overlook something or make a mistake. Instead of crucifying ourselves when we fall short, revelling in the guilt, we should instead try to shift the gear from self-destruction to owning and learning from our mistakes, bouncing back from a setback, building the resilience muscle, and being faster in our recovery. This is the example I try to set for my daughter.

Raising my daughter to feel safe, valued and loved, no matter what, is the most important parenting thing I have ever been able to do. I hope I have played a small part in making her feel special, cherished and respected for her incredible strengths and uniqueness. To know that she is her own person. Sometimes that comes from an impromptu hug, other times, from providing a listening ear without judgement, more often than not, from providing simple encouragement to be fearless and independent in taking decisions, and to allow some margin for error.

My daughter is the epitome of smart, funny and beautiful. She is humanity itself and earth is a better place with her in it. I want her to always know she is good enough.

I AM ME

I am me
Happy in this skin
Content with myself
At peace in my own company
Relishing what gifts each day brings
Embracing the unknown future with open arms
Excited to share my thoughts with the world
Proud I have something important to say
Accepting of my past
For it shaped me
Into who I am
I am me

So, if you are like me and you don't nail this parenting business anywhere close to 100% of the time, cut yourself a break.

The point is to love unconditionally. To be humble in the receipt of success and graceful and accepting in the face of defeat. If we can't give ourselves permission to drop the ball and make mistakes, then our kids are going to forever strive for the unattainable, hanging their hat and self-worth on a paralysing goal of perfectionism.

Giving your undivided attention, quality time and whole heart to your daughter are some of the most valuable gifts you can offer. They are the secret ingredients of a recipe that will empower them to celebrate their strengths, accept their flaws and live fearlessly.

STARGAZER MOMENT

*You are the apple
of my eye, but I won't try
to die-cast myself.*

- Always let your daughter know that you love her unconditionally and that 'she is enough'.
- Encourage her to have opinions of her own and a voice in making decisions.
- Find ways to problem-solve independently or as a family rather than you solving everything on behalf of everyone else.
- Identify the things your daughter loves and encourage her to pursue them wholeheartedly.
- Don't overly shelter your daughter. Allow 'risk-taking' from an early age. Physical playtime in the dirt or climbing a tree is just as good for girls as it is for boys.
- Teach a 'fail fast' lesson rather than 'don't fail' and avoid putting on your superhero cape to swoop in on the struggle too soon to save the day.
- Be selfish with your time and avoid spreading yourself too thin.
- Pick and choose what you commit to as a parent, then invest your whole self into being present in the moment.
- Allow self-expression and embrace uniqueness – don't try to create a mini carbon copy of yourself.

- Throw up the balls and juggle with varied levels of competency.
- When you inevitably drop something, bounce back faster and stronger than before.

What can you do to improve the quality of time spent with your daughter?

_____

_____

_____

_____

What positive, uplifting message can you give your daughter next time you see her?

_____

_____

_____

_____

When you drop the parenting ball, what positive advice can you give yourself?

_____

_____

_____

_____

_____

_____

V
SUN

We have a boy too. A film-making genius who turns my literary word into a flick that does the trick of conveying my hard-hitting messages to an audience I want to influence into changing the world for the better.

Together he and I think not outside the box but like there is no box as we look past blue sky to infinity and beyond. He puts lights, camera, action on my poetic verse trying to reverse the generational cycle of the underdog to instil resilience and brilliance in the lost children seeking a working-class revolution. And I'm proud of him for making me look at life through the next-gen millennial lens of a person trying to shine the light on the plight of humanity.

This is my sun.

Growing up, I recall being confused on what I wanted to eventually do for a job. There was no career advisory service at school. No information sessions hosted about how to become 'work ready'. It was a straightforward case of figuring it out for oneself.

I had a few different ideas. I delved into work experience for a week with the British Army and absolutely loved the adrenaline, physical activity and structured ways of the military. Then, when I wanted to enlist, my teacher discouraged me, citing that service life was not a job for 'girls'. I thought about other options. Working in an office, doing whatever job I could where I would have regular income and be a bona fide professional or becoming a war journalist. And at the age of thirteen I declared to my two best friends that I would one day write a novel.

Today, I work on large defence contracts in the corporate world. I remain inspired and in awe of the amazing serving personnel who are courageously committed to defending others.

I am also the bestselling author of multiple books and have had my work published across a long list of international media outlets. Somehow, I have ended up right where I was always meant to be.

I also mentor youths from lower socio-economic backgrounds, encouraging them to chase their dreams wholeheartedly and to never give up when faced with a roadblock.

Every child is different and deserved of being given a chance in life. If your child wants to be an astronaut one day, I encourage you to avoid jumping straight into thinking it may be unattainable. Instead, take them to the planetarium to gaze at the stars or buy them a book about the wonders of the solar system.

The sun is a plasma ball of heat and light, sustaining life on earth as its most important source of incandescent energy.

It is the radiant star right at the heart of the solar system, shining as a bright beacon to guide the rest of the world.

STARING AT THE SUN

It is impossible to draw
the gazing away
from the amazing
energy at play.

One day, sometime in his early teens, my son declared out of nowhere that he wanted to write his own scripts and become a film director to bring them to the screen. My husband and I encouraged him to watch a broad range of movies, from old classics to the latest blockbuster releases. He got stuck into working his way through whole back catalogues from certain iconic directors, checking out their different techniques and styles. Evenings disappeared into subtitled foreign films. Weekends were spent absorbed in black-and-white silent movies. He made a short film for a school project that won him his first award and in his late teens won Best Actor, Best Cinematography and Best Film in a New South Wales Film Festival and his first short movie played on the big screen in a local cinema.

He has never looked back.

He majored in film and English at university and has since had books of his own published. He likes nothing better than writing his own scripts, penned with a narrative of strong underlying social conscience weaving a golden thread. In his spare time, he spends endless hours either behind the camera or editing raw footage into his vision of a cinematic masterpiece.

Just like the sun, my son creates his own nuclear fusions that react together in an explosion of positive energy that fuels and sustains others in its glowing nucleus.

No two boys are alike, but you can teach all boys alike to appreciate and pursue the things that are important to him.

Encourage your boys to be willing to work hard to chase a big hairy audacious goal and to be unwavering in the belief that it can be achieved. You can coach the development of a growth mindset that sets high personal standards, instil respect and help establish an inner psychology of putting values at the heart and to wear them on the sleeve.

Challenge your son to observe what is going on with a 'fisheye lens' on the camera, widening the perspective beyond what is in the immediate sphere.

And when he is old enough, talk to him about current affairs that seem to tug at his heartstrings, cultivating concern for others so he can find purpose and meaning in the interests he develops.

The endless conversations I have with my son about all manner of weird and wonderful topics are precious moments to forever hold sacred. They have forged a bond between us that bridges childhood into adulthood through taking the time to understand what truly makes his mind tick.

I want my son to always know this of himself:

FIRST PLACE

While so many race
to chase first place
you make the world
a better place.

It can be difficult raising children, and it is certainly not all plain sailing. The great moments need to be cherished and fed air supply, so they reproduce and overshadow the more challenging moments.

Watch what makes your child smile, observe their passions, listen to them intently and encourage them to try new things. Allow experimentation rather than be disheartened if they change their mind. Most kids don't know what they want to be and that is okay.

It's important to recognise there are many different pathways to success, not all of them academic, and forcing our children to fit a certain mould or comparing them to others more often than not can fail to produce a good outcome.

As parents, we often have sky-high aspirations for our children and want them to be successful and happy in their skin. Paying genuine attention to the things that matter to them, affirming their efforts, allowing them to follow individual paths that are right for them and being a strong ethical role model in our own behaviours will help them develop a positive mentality.

Let your children flourish and lead a fulfilling life that impacts themselves and others for the better.

STARGAZER MOMENT

*If we are all unique
we are all the same.
If we are all the same
I want to be unique.*

- Idiosyncrasy in our children is good or the world would become a very boring place for us all.
- Encourage exploration, expand perspective and stimulate curiosity.
- Nurture new ideas and be a role model for innovative thinking.
- Provide opportunities for creative expression.
- Foster an open mindset and demonstrate positive thinking so it has a knock-on effect to those around you.
- Read to your child, watch different movies from the mainstream recommendations, allow for unstructured playtime.
- Experiment different experiences; watch for the spark in their eye and that moment that triggers a beaming smile to creep in.
- Allow for a change of direction, normalise failures and celebrate successes.
- Support your children unconditionally in exploring their weird and wonderful ideas and aspirations.
- Help your child to be socially aware, which will help facilitate the development of a positive attitude and moral sense of purpose early in life.

How can you further encourage your son and support him in the pursuit of his passions?

_____

_____

_____

_____

Are there any new techniques you can try to gently nudge your son to step outside of his comfort zone?

_____

_____

_____

_____

When you next sit down to chat to your son about his hopes and dreams, what will you say?

_____

_____

_____

_____

_____

VI
SATURN

Then there's the pinstripe age when I'm out of family range, driving organisational change years after paving the way from unionised pay to make hay at the top of the corporate ladder. The girl from the street who wanted to beat the odds stacked against her, combatting perpetuating education elitism with determination and realism in my vocation.

I broke every rule when I became a mule, smuggling under-aged innocence and any lack of brilliance beneath feigned self-confidence, running rings around the competition, on a mission to be the best version of me and always helping others to be free in their thinking. This ring of ambitious fire is my pattern.

This is my Saturn.

Whenever you think about Saturn, I hope you visualise its unique adornment of thousands of beautiful ringlets. It is the taskmaster planet of ambition, tenacity, productivity, concentration, tangible rewards and permanence.

Saturn is also the astonishingly clever planet that rules responsibility, fear, pain, discipline and control. The deeper you delve, the more it gets steadily warmer, denser and the pressure builds. Nobody can stand up on Saturn, but isn't that a compelling enough reason to knock people off their feet?

Saturn is spectacularly complicated, and what is not to like about that?

I was thirteen years old when I began working part-time on Saturdays and had barely turned sixteen when I got my first full-time office job. Taking on full-time work happened as a result of dropping out of sixth form A-levels to earn my keep, with half of my wages immediately handed over to my mother to contribute towards rent and food.

Like most people entering employment at an early age, I started out on the very bottom rung of the ladder, at a small family-owned stamp, coin and military medals auctioneering company. Daily tasks involved sorting out the mail, keeping the office tidy and doing basic administration. The team made me feel welcome and I felt extremely grateful for being given such a fantastic opportunity to work in such a pleasant and unusual environment.

Being the best version of oneself does not have to be costly. At the time, I possessed only a single decent black skirt and a couple of smart shirts, but I dressed the part, always as neatly turned out as I could be, and I was always polite, hard-working and on time, even though I was a night owl who barely slept.

Respect starts with yourself before it translates to others. I did not want to reflect the mess at home, or let myself down, and I certainly did not want to let down any of the friendly and professional colleagues I worked with at the auctioneers. They had given me the best starting chance of going from the bottom of the ladder to the second step and I was not going to slip off the rung.

Being on time may sound like a basic given, but me and time have always endured a very complicated love-hate relationship.

On the one hand, I greatly value every minute of being awake. As an action-oriented person, filling my days to the brim with enriching activities is normal practice. It is rare that I sit idle and even if I am enjoying a quiet walk with the dog or a spot of sunbathing on a beach holiday, my brain is generally geared into overdrive, plotting my next mission.

On the other hand, through conscious perseverance, I have, over many years, managed to adapt healthier sleep patterns that go somewhat towards killing off my insomnia. I generally feel physically better and more energised by getting more regular sleep, but the loss of productivity from those extra hours in the day can still niggle away at my thoughts and feel like an irritant if I let it.

I easily digress into my old bad sleep habits if I do not maintain the discipline I've managed to adopt over the years. I have to consciously combat not just the insomnia itself, but also find ways to still fit in all the things I want to do with my day.

While I never want to compromise family and I made a pact with myself a long time ago to always give 110% at work, without some good time management strategies, my creative writing would be the thing that would no doubt be eroded. I've found ways to overcome this through finding new ways of maximising shorter time slots I have at my disposal.

WORK TO LIVE

When did I forget to work to live,
not to live to work, nor take more than give

back to others, sisters and brothers
needing my help and the help of others

to get back on their feet, giving heart steady beat,
looking back on the past to pay it forward.

Over the last couple of years, I have been recording haiku poems on my voice app instead of penning longer pieces. These short, sharp poems have found a whole new social media audience who prefer to consume snappy pieces instead of devouring essay-length pieces. I've taken to plotting new book ideas while walking the dog. And I try to keep flight times sacred for writing longer pieces like working on the chapters of a novel. Working at 35,000 feet always seems to work well for churning out a good chunk of prose. Long live the days of no internet on the majority of aircraft.

I've also found ways to improve how I multitask, which like any other new integral skill, needs building up with practice. Good multitasking commands decent cognitive resources and has meant developing heightened attention to detail and keeping the wheels of memory well-oiled to turn around the clock. Everyone has quite an impressive inner capability to self-activate resources to meet increased demands. Once our brain achieves that higher level of activation, it generates extra energy which can be used in different ways, stimulating cognitive flexibility.

Most people have a remarkable ability to multitask. In fact, mastering multitasking, whilst it should not be habitual, is a necessity now more than ever before as the ever-evolving world becomes faster in pace. More and more parents of all genders opt to balance both careers, children, hobbies, hustles and passions. While there will only ever be twenty-four hours in any given day, often thirty hours of activity management is needed.

Multitasking is the ability to simultaneously perform more than one task, without compromising speed, quality or performance too much.

There are, of course, times when tasks should not be blended. Obvious situations crop up where it would pose too much of a risk if we were to have even the slightest reduction of 100% attention on one activity. For example, making phone calls while driving the car is off limits.

But there are times when it can be hugely beneficial to toggle between a few things at once so we can be more productive.

NO TIME LIKE THE PRESENT

                If I

left

        everything to be done
        one thing at a time
        I would never get to

                              write

Multitasking sounds easy enough, but it can be a complicated process, and it has its pitfalls. Our brains are not necessarily neatly wired to immediately know when to complete more than one task at a time, and no two human brains are the same. We may lack the natural instinct to perform simultaneous tasks at the same level of efficiency and performance as if running a solo task, but with practise and dedication, we can develop cognitive control to task-manage to the best of our abilities so we avoid negatively deteriorating the quality outcome of whatever it is we are trying to accomplish.

Whilst it may indeed be impossible for every individual to truly achieve the gold standard on absolutely everything, if you chose to multitask, there are some techniques for training your brain that will go towards mastering the art of managing multiple tasks simultaneously.

These start with setting goals and ensuring you have a plan designed to achieve them, otherwise you will end up with goals that dwindle into nothing but a dream drifting along on a wing and a prayer.

To have the best chance of gaining more benefit than risk from multitasking requires you to succinctly focus your attention on where it is most impactful. Optimising your efforts in those priority areas aligned to your aspirations, whether it is for work, family, relationships or personal satisfaction, will ensure you accomplish your goals faster.

DEADLINE

The race is on
Too slow off the mark
Already losing to bitter foe
Time cocooned within invisible cloak
Weaved from relentless pressure

A perpetual rush
Angst jumbles clarity of thought
Unyielding iron grip
Mind evades prioritisation
Repudiates common sense
Spawning chronic tightness of gut

Xerostomia develops in mouth barren of saliva
Forehead frown etches into deep gully
Damp patch spreads under armpits
Perspiration trickles down back
Wipe damp hands down pinstripe jacket
Rub grit from weary eyes
Heart races from excessive caffeine
Brain scrambles to decipher demands

Create one-page plan
Apply logic to priorities
Delegate non-critical components
Remove grey ambiguity
Administer prescriptive black and white instructions
Track progress with colourful traffic lights
Manage outcomes with clenched iron fist
Punch the deadline

If you consciously ensure the things you're working on are those that bring you the most value and are stepping stones to more rapidly pave the way to your goals, you will by default find it easier to say no to wasting unnecessary energy on the wrong activities just to appease others.

You will be less tempted to overcomplicate what you are working on at any one time, so you are not overwhelmed by projects or tasks that meet the needs of others but overshadow your own or burdens you with additional stress.

Simplification of tasks into straightforward bite-sized chunks that are aligned to moving you a notch towards your identified goals will help you to stay on point. Knocking them off one by one in a more systematic manner will eventually become habit.

You can also drive simplicity by combining similar tasks to work on alongside those that have synergies. This will avoid wasting time switching between different threads and will help train your brain to remain on point.

Minimising a wandering mind is key to success. It is essential you eliminate distractions which can be the detrimental enemy of multitasking. Establish the right working conditions that feed your productivity, for example quiet, bright space with good ergonomics. Set your sights on what you need to achieve, consistently look back to review your activity to ensure you are not bleeding precious efforts and your labours are ticking boxes aligned to your overarching goals.

Structure your day according to what works best for you. I tend to tackle the more difficult agenda items in the morning when I am at my freshest, so they don't linger unfinished for too long. Once the painful stuff is out of the way, the whole day looks a whole lot brighter.

I call this 'eat the frog'.

EAT THE FROG

Hop
onto
to-do-list
bright eyes bulging
no time to relax
croaking on lily pad
soaked in slimy denial
pretend it's another's poison
until finally the time comes round
to swallow excuses and eat the frog.

Another useful technique to improve your multitasking capability is to combine complex and mindless tasks. Structure your day to ringfence quality time on the more complicated activities that require the ultimate focus, such as attending and paying attention in key meetings, working on business strategy, completing a training course or kicking off the first draft of that novel you always wanted to write.

Balance these with churning out low-brainpower tasks like doing the ironing, cooking or taking the dog for a walk. Pair up mindless and complex tasks to conduct together, for example, hold a one-to-one work meeting while walking the dog or listen to a corporate podcast while doing the ironing. Doubling down on your output in this way can bring an extraordinary sense of satisfaction.

If you find yourself doubting that it is worth the effort, grab onto the gentle reminder that in today's society, multitasking is a valuable asset that can be used to your advantage. It is a skill valued by employers who expect teams to be able to balance competing demands.

There are very few jobs, if any, that allow an employee the luxury of focusing on one linear task at a time. We must be able to rotate our concentration silently and smoothly and be cognisant of competing priorities. We have to demonstrate the ability to run multiple projects, achieve a plethora of service levels, smash several targets, interact with a wide range of stakeholders, rub our heads and pat our stomachs, all while drinking a large skimmed flat white because someone double-booked the diary straight through morning tea break.

There are obvious intersections between stress and poor time management, so it is important to recognise those moments when you are not on top of things and need to adjust the calendar to take time out. Do not feel guilty for wanting to protect your basic needs such as taking in the right nutrition and having a good night's sleep.

If you need to go for a walk to clear the head, curl up with a good book or veg out on the sofa to binge-watch a mini-series, let yourself indulge in the urge. We generally function at our best when our own mental health is nurtured and cared for.

We are all human, with different goals, unique strengths and a variety of weaknesses. No brain is limitless, but each of us has the ability to develop the skill of multitasking through ongoing perseverance and commitment to creating a positive mindset.

You owe it to yourself to be the best version of yourself possible and to achieve everything your destiny commands of you.

STARGAZER MOMENT

No prize for second best
so don't rest
in the quest
to be first
against yourself.

- Keep your family, friends, health and wellbeing front of mind and at the top of your list.
- Know what you want to achieve and be selfish in your plan of attack.
- Be tenacious in aiming to be the best at what you do.
- Avoid being overwhelmed by prioritising what is important and by tacking things with a cool head in an orderly, organised fashion.
- Combine a schedule of thoughtful tasks that require higher levels of focus and mindless tasks that require little to no brain power to complete.
- Eat the frog – avoid procrastination. Stay calm and face into the tasks that are most urgent or complex in the first half of the day when your brain is at its most refreshed.
- Complete more mundane tasks that allow you to operate on autopilot later in the day.
- Assign time limits and take breaks as working continuously without coming up for air will drain you and inevitably reduce the quality of your output.

- Be fearless in your efforts and face into mistakes to uncover the learnings, for the more we fail, the more resilient we become.
- If you find you have taken on too much and are dropping the ball so often you are becoming angry, depressed, ineffective or overly stressed, review your goals and rethink your strategy to refocus on what is most important and make necessary adjustments in your life.
- You owe it to yourself to selfishly pursue your dreams and know that you are worthy of success.

What is your long-term ambition in life and what are the next steps you can take to achieve this?

_____

_____

_____

_____

List your short-term goals for the year ahead and begin creating an action plan that aligns your priorities to them.

_____

_____

_____

_____

How can you create the conditions for success so you can be the best version of yourself?

VII
MOON

Then the darkness sets in and the side hustle kicks in as I morph into a poet with deeply rooted scars engrained in a sonnet, sharing verse overflowing with what's real, helping to heal this soul who broke and was put back together on an open mic, baring every crack in the spotlight, not caring if this poem is filled with so many loose threads it can never be wound on a spool, because I'm still the goddamn sharpest tool in the box that you can't box me into, because I'll always be the girl who broke every rule in the school who grew into a woman who would rather rhyme to make a dime than recline and decline back into old school. So here I am, hands shaking, facade breaking, these words of truth leaving my tonsils raw and my heart ... on the floor, exhausted from this stanza bonanza, my face beaming with adrenaline as I cut through the darkness with the neon starkness of truth.

This is my moon.

(Please, no need to swoon that I'm the first woman to land on the moon as I certainly won't be the last.)

Like many writers, I have had a love affair with books for as long as I can remember.

In my teens, as well as being an avid fiction reader, I also loved immersing myself into the written student assignments for school English lessons. I aspired to be a non-fiction writer or a war journalist and harboured the ambition of publishing a book. I knew it was possible and never doubted I would find a way to achieve this dream. Amidst all of my ideas was the notion that words could capture the moment of the here and now and log it forever so it would never be lost. I understood the magical powers held in each sentence that allowed someone to teleport mentally to someplace else.

During my twenties, I turned to poetry, embracing freestyle techniques and contemporary short form verse as a way to process recollections of childhood which I had buried for years. I could take part in this silent therapy alone and on the move, jotting down pieces in short sharp bursts that I found liberating. I filled notebooks with scribbled ideas and began compiling works in progress.

My thirties brought along a new desire to refine my craft as a fiction author, chewing on forbidden fruits, tasting the distaste and swallowing the pips of the taboo, never spitting the unsavoury out. Evenings were spent working on a darker style of short story, scaling into months pulling together a whole collection. It took years and years of drafting and re-drafting my first novel, *The Pinstripe Prisoner*. Although I was still unpublished during this era, this was the raw phase where I truly immersed myself in writing and began to appreciate the subtleties of character building and the value of disciplined editing.

In my forties, life began to get even more crazy. I mean really crazy. It became a juncture of tasks, navigating meetings, creating to-do lists, organising places I needed to be and people I needed to see. Work had turned me into a workaholic, where self-care and wellness were tossed out the window. Without intervention, this unhealthy pattern would have become irreversibly overwhelming. Debilitating as it paralysed the brain, or conversely for me, perversely over-stimulated the mind, disabling any possible notion I might have of falling asleep and getting a half-decent amount of shut-eye.

During this workaholic phase, I continued to use words to calm the tsunami. To unwind from the day's corporate madness, I wrote late at night, always before bed after everyone else in our house was snoring their heads off. The creative cogs of my brain seemed to click into motion at an even faster pace, my pen travelling over paper at an accelerated pace, fuelled by the day's observations and pressures.

I rewrote the novel I had been working on for a decade and submitted it to various literary agents. I have more than fifty rejection letters to reflect on, but I kept on going, taking on the constructive criticism to try and improve my next piece of writing.

Eventually, I got signed up by the Newman Agency, who read my novel and thought it worthy of publication.

I also took a good look at the hundreds of poems from floppy disks, hard drives, USB sticks and notebooks and grouped them into themes. It gave me enough material to cherry-pick from to put into my first poetry collection.

And I dropped in a few more short story submissions to writing competitions and took the gong on a few.

It was my contemporary poetry that got published first. A publisher took me under her wing and my debut poetry book, *Graffiti Lane*, was born.

Suddenly, I was caught in the headlights as *Graffiti Lane* took off and rose to bestseller status. The peacefulness of writing with abandonment late at night became exposed in a more challenging phase. My diary rapidly filled up, not only with the usual schedule of corporate strategy planning, customer visits, team meetings and budget sessions, but also the evenings began to get jammed with dealing with media enquiries, TV and radio interviews, author talks and requests to be the feature poet at major spoken word events.

I was in my forties when I first took to the open mic to perform poetry live. It was daunting. Putting yourself out there in front of a bunch of strangers. Poetry is deeply personal, and I found it harder to do than any keynote speech I have ever had to give. Yet living outside of the comfort zone, trying something new like slam poetry, was somewhat liberating. I was living on the edge. Going to new venues. Meeting new people. Using a part of my toolkit that had never been given any kind of trial run. And like anything, practise began to make perfect. The events got bigger. I won a few slams. Dropped a few mics. Forgot my words a couple of times. Practised harder.

Little did I know, all of those hours on the open mic, which moved into the online poetry circuit during COVID-19, were the perfect training for what later would become my twelve-minute TEDx talk, delivered in poetic verse.

My writing became all-consuming. There were not enough hours in the day to take a bathroom break, let alone write another book. What was once beautiful, creative, private space was suddenly eroded.

Any glimpse of spare time was spent sitting on the sidelines at my daughter's netball matches, operating as a taxi driver to wherever my two teenagers were dashing off to and making sure there was a hot freshly cooked meal on the table. My husband and I would try to respectively book in our work travel with a new level of precision coordination, sanitising our schedules to make sure we avoided overlapping. Every meeting was meticulously booked into the online calendar, yet I would open up the diary each morning and find appointments were double- or triple-booked.

I was dropping the ball more than I was catching it.

I became the mother who forgot the oranges at netball and had to compensate a whole team of hungry girls with a bag of jelly snakes. I was the embarrassed parent who got red cheeks when I turned up at kid's parties on the wrong day. I was that scatty woman who accidently left her handbag under the table at the local cafe at least once a week.

In recent years, during these fabulous forties, I began writing non-fiction for community impact and positive purpose. Several articles got published about the long-term socio-economic impacts of unemployment, education elitism, bullying, domestic violence, mental health, substance abuse, suicide. Often, I interject these shorter pieces with a perspective on the benefits of grassroots programs, the rise of predictive analytics for crime prevention or the need for ongoing prison reform to reduce recidivism.

PARALYSIS BUSTER

Hope is not a strategy,
but it stimulates
a shift from paralysis
to bold action
to get traction.

81% of people say they want to write a book but never do it. 15% make a start. 6% reach the halfway house. 3% finish a first draft. 0.6% make it to publication.

It may have taken me a couple of decades of refining my craft before I was signed up by a literary agent, but this has shaped who I am as an author. I still reflect on feedback, good and bad, and have morphed my craft accordingly. No written piece of mine goes anywhere without six rounds of end-to-end editing on my part. Many projects I start get binned. Others get filed away to collect dust for a while, until they are given a new lease of life. Yet, that dream I had at thirteen years old of writing a book became a reality.

Never give up.

The most common reason running through rejection letters I have received over the years has been around the notion that my work is a hybrid of genres. Seemingly, I cannot be pigeon-holed onto a singular commercial bookshelf – of fiction, non-fiction, traditional poetry or prose. Nobody knows quite exactly where to put me on the bookshelf.

I have made past attempts to respond to this feedback to be a popular genre, easily labelled author, by writing a crime book. This failed miserably in the category of 'filed under dust'. Then I turned my hand to prescriptive, traditional stanza as it is so much easier to define the audience. These attempts made the halfway house. I scribbled some bubble-gum romance that in theory would be easier to market than a confused poet, come fiction writer, come social justice non-fiction advocate. These meagre attempts hit the trash can.

Sticking to a single genre held little to no appeal for me. I like to break rigid rules and unleash creative license.

So, I quit trying to conform and went back to my earliest objectives around reshaping the status quo:

- Rewrite the blueprint.
- Break the mould.
- Smash through glass ceilings.

While I like to span different genres, the one consistent theme in everything I have produced is that I always write about urban life and current influences on society today. I love to play with contrasts. The darker side of the mind grappling in equal measures with willpower, tenacity, ambition, honesty, humility and hope.

I experiment whenever I can, fusing written work with street photography and commissioned illustrations. Some time ago I began dabbling with kinetic typography to create movement in otherwise two-dimensional words. Worked with my son to create short movies from my poems for various literary festivals. Dipped my toe into platform poetry, posting haikus on Instagram and Twitter. Went alone to the open mic nights and tried to improve my slam poetry rhythm. Began recording new work on my voice app while walking the dog. Put together the TEDx speech in poetic verse.

I gave up trying to force myself to become someone I am not.

It is a gift to oneself to think not outside the box, but like there is no box and to live with the freedom of no frame.

I began to explore the notion of authenticity, where failures counted just as much, if not more, than successes.

Our failures are often the foundations of our growth. Our strengths can be our weaknesses and our weaknesses our strengths. The good in us all is interconnected and interdependent with the bad. Everything idiosyncratic we are made up of matters.

Hang-ups from childhood have at times brought out the worst of me. They have also given me steely resilience that is my ultimate superpower, more so, perhaps, than the fizzing energy. Resilience means finding the mechanisms to cope in spite of barriers, climbing over obstacles and taking one step forward, even if at times we have been forced to take two steps back.

This abundance of resilience has been embedded in a sturdy belief that it is possible to reframe the norms. It is something I draw upon to combat the toughest of environments or deal with the aftermath of an unexpected clash.

Conflict can stimulate something good.

After all, the moon was likely formed after a Mars-sized body collided with earth. Instead of fragmenting from this head-on impact, something beautiful was formed.

What goes up, must come down.

Complimenting Yin is the contrary force of Yang.

In darkness we find light.

A four-line poem from my debut book, *Graffiti Lane,* captures the essence of this.

SHATTERED

*What once shattered me
into a million pieces
is now what makes me
razor sharp.*

The result of bucking the single-genre author trends by fusing different literary forms was the spawning of an entirely new audience. I am most grateful that my raw and gritty style found its way to a wide and varied audience, from at-risk youths, to street artists, to corporate leaders, Oscar winners, political figureheads and royalty.

Writing is the Yin that fills my nights. It is the black layers of authenticity and a complex character shrouded by a dark past. It is the quiet force of creativity dancing in the shadows of the moon, where death is on the horizon only because of a fully celebrated life. It is the softness of exposed soul and the cold, hard, raw truth of thoughts and words collated into idealisms that are deeply engrained and everlasting.

The white of Yang, on the other hand, symbolises warmth. The positive fizz of energy injected into day-to-day work, filled with active motion and seared with the heat of the sun. Corporate dedication and altruism shine through actions, backed up with considered choices and logical thinking, hard work and hot passion to succeed in the mission. It is the birth of new ideas to propel others forward and the affirmation gifted to myself and others so that individually and collectively we make a meaningful difference to society and the world we inhabit.

These traits amalgamate in a hybrid blend of Yin and Yang, powered by the sustenance that is family, friends, my tribal community and network.

Over the last quarter of a century, I have been deeply embedded in the Yang of the business world. During the years of my earlier career, work was all-consuming, overshadowing creative aspirations and brutally cutting into quality family time.

In 2014, I was privileged to be sent to IMD, a world-class business school, based in Lausanne, Switzerland. During my residency, highly customised, extreme learning techniques were implemented in indoor settings as well as in the outdoors of the Swiss Alps. These were designed to:

- Explore past influences and triggers.
- Develop mindfulness techniques.
- Challenge the status quo and inspire what could be in the future.

This was a turning point for me. An opportunity to unpack the excess baggage, toss away several heavy boulders and repack the luggage for the long-haul. My passport was stamped with a fresh outlook, the destination was open-ended. Prescriptive instructions were given to cease feeling like a tourist in my own life. Each session gave expressed permission to stop spreading efforts too thin. To selfishly say no to things without feeling guilty.

My lesson was to try and work at 90% rather than 110% and to shed the constant personal pressure of trying to be all things to all people.

For the first time, I was told to put myself first sometimes and to abolish the need to constantly prove to others that despite leaving school at sixteen, I was good enough.

Absolution through affirmation and through poetry to heal my own trauma does not mean the inherent desire to serve others disappears. Only that it is not at the detriment of self-preservation and personal growth. The desire to make things better for others remains integral to my ideals of happiness.

Life presents many opportunities where we can unselfishly impact another person positively.

Serving others, whether it be as an author, a mentor, in business circles or through community initiatives, is an honour and a privilege that should never be taken for granted. It doesn't require a degree in social sciences or a platinum bank account. Just the concept that preserving oneself with a healthy dose of self-love and self-forgiveness can provide the important linkage into showing kindness and empathy towards others. So much joy can be found in giving to others with a humble heart.

When you do something selfless for someone else, it comes back tenfold, often changing your life, and theirs, from the inside out.

Despite these best intentions, I am still prone to saying yes to more than I should. Energy ends up getting spread too thin, diluting running power, so batteries need recharging before they run dry. There are times when helping others is a non-negotiable and other times when stepping back and pausing to self-invest in personal wellbeing is the sensible move.

There are also occasions when it is still the right thing to do to attend an event you really don't feel like going to, because you love the person hosting it and you want to make the ones you love happy. And other times when you should be selfish in clawing the time back or when it is okay to steer clear because that negative person who drains your last bar of energy is going to be there.

For many people, being able to say no can be an adjustment, especially if you are the pleasing type prone to always saying yes. Saying no sometimes will invariably serve yourself, and often others, better in the long run. By delving into conscious thinking when a request comes your way, you can begin to identify scenarios where it is best to say no, at the right moment and in the right way.

OXYGEN

*Put your oxygen mask on first
before quenching the thirst
of others.*

While I was up in the Swiss Alps, in addition to being coached to say no a bit more often, I also confronted my inner critic. The irritating one that would all too often prod away at my psyche to tell me I was the working-class underdog. I tackled it with the affirmation weapon of:

I am good enough.

Engraining this reframed perspective into cognitive thinking has not been easy, so I now draw upon one other phrase to add to my affirmation kit bag.

It is a quote I once heard from a former boss of mine, way back in the days of my early career.

WE ALL HAVE WINGS

*Only you
can spread your wings
and fly.*

This phrase serves as a reminder that to hold oneself back or propel ourselves forward is a choice we make. Let imposter syndrome and the demands of the social system bind us as a hostage or set ourselves free to fly the cuckoo's nest. Clip our own wings or let ourselves soar to new heights.

We have all the power we need within ourselves to ensure self-doubt does not paralyse the body and mind. To take strength from the darkness, enabling us to leverage the divine essence of our beings, creating the energy source of all light and life within us. To exist at an even higher level than our souls and be everything we can be. To embrace the Yin and Yang of everything that makes us whole and allow light and darkness to coexist.

I choose to write without boundaries. Break rules that serve no ongoing purpose. Grow as a leader. Reward others. Collectively celebrate business wins. Learn from mistakes made on the job. Selfishly indulge in quality time with my husband, kids and dog doing the things we love. Welcome new opportunities with open arms.

Live a life on my terms without regrets.

There are too many lessons I've learned over the years to recount even a small fraction of them in this book. Undoubtedly there are a zillion I can't even remember, let alone recite, but there are a select bunch that have stuck with me to form my personal perspective, professional foundations, and moral compass.

At some point, I came to realise that the only way I could fill the void pages of a new non-fiction book was to embrace authenticity and write about what I know, from direct experience and from the heart. This could not be curtailed to sticking to one topic of writing, whether it be business, or motherhood, or marriage, or writing, for individually they each represent only a portion of me. In fact, this book turned out to not only be non-fiction, but contemporary poetry too. Cross-genre fist pump!

- Rules can be broken.
- Boundaries can be crossed.
- Genres can be merged.

This means killing my own radiation. Terminating the things that have been holding me back from putting pen to paper. Exterminating the voice at the back of my mind telling me to stick to popular topics and remain in my comfort zone. Ignoring the naysayers who drill it into authors that it's impossible to successfully cross-pollinate literary genres. Being unafraid of not being right for a whole audience because maybe it is possible to reach at least one. And that is worth it.

I implore you to do the same. Take a chance and abolish all notions of playing it safe and staying in your lane.

STARGAZER MOMENT

*It's fine to say no
to create space to say yes
to progress.*

- When approached by someone for something, listen, learn, talk, but resist the urge to dive in and immediately agree. Instead let them know you will get back to them after you have had time to properly consider the request.
- Reduce psychological pressure to instantly say yes by creating physical distance away from the requester to think through the ask.
- Create the headspace and time to decide if you should say no or cave in to duty and say yes, in which case consider if you will have to reprioritise other commitments and what you will have to compromise to make it happen.
- Call, email or have a face-to-face conversation if you decide it is best to turn down a request for assistance. Look for any ideas or suggestions for alternatives or suggest simple assistance options such as providing a link to online resources. These can be a great way to make the conversation easier for those who cannot shake off the guilt when saying no to something.
- Do a mental check and embrace the courageous decision to constructively say no rather than letting guilt clutter your valuable head space.

- Ignore the sense of rejection of someone saying no to you and embrace the moment as a stretch opportunity to be innovative and self-sufficient.
- Break free from the status quo and allow your creativity to flourish in new directions that surprise the hell out of yourself.
- Challenge the thought process, even your own. There are no physical boundaries in decision-making.
- Explore different choices with abandonment.

When did you last say yes against your better judgement, what made you over-commit, and what can you learn from it?

_____

_____

_____

_____

If you could carve an hour out of your day, how would you indulgently use it to your benefit or joy?

_____

_____

_____

_____

When someone next says no to you, how can you turn the disappointment on its head?

VIII
KRYPTON

Eventually an eclipse came when a collision of parallel lives caused an unsustainable landslide while I tried to hide behind a superhero mask sewn with pride, as I tried to fly and fly and fly so high I could well see papa in heaven's sky, instead crash landing on unfamiliar territory barren of fellow human race, no longer protected by a Kevlar cape keeping my psyche safe from Kryptonite bullets fired at the escape route back to my true identity.

How many of us are trying to conform to the norm? Aiming to reform to take the world by storm. Attempting to transform into the clone society demands we become. In the process of acquiring skills expected of a senior executive, building up agility and capability around strategy and risk and behavioural DISC, craters had formed in my integrity. It was time to abort being a pocket rocket, packing my luggage of courage into a NASA rocket launching into space to a place where I could tenaciously embrace my flaws because I'm not, never have been, never will be, never want to be Superwoman. It's time to leave this side of the mind behind with the Kryptonite.

This is my Krypton.

Krypton was a fictional planet created by DC. It was populated by a great civilisation of scientifically advanced Kryptonians, who developed enhanced physical characteristics, including an injection of super-strength and agility. An explosion destructed the planet but not before two talented scientists were able to co-design evacuation spaceships that would transport their children to safety on earth. These children would eventually grow up to become the renowned superheroes, Superman and Power Girl.

Like most things, 100% perfection is never the reality, hence radioactive fragments of the planet remained in the atmosphere and are known as Kryptonite.

The majority of us have some kind of deeply rooted sense of place that stems from childhood. This can amalgamate into fond nostalgic memories of happiness. Or it can explode and lodge radioactive shards of Kryptonite into your subconsciousness.

Throughout childhood, I lived in a council house on an estate riddled with unemployment and crime. The police helicopter regularly circled over the rooftops, beams on, trying to lock the joyriders into the spotlight. The blues were always flashing, sirens loudly proclaiming the presence of law and order to supress the ongoing antisocial behaviour of residents.

Friends lived for the thrill of the crime, with jail time seen as a badge of honour. Others began glue-sniffing as kids and died as teens from harder narcs addiction. Some were murdered for messing with the wrong gang. Mostly, though, we all shared the commonality of navigating tough circumstances.

We were the imperfect children, some of us good, some bad.

All of us were trying to make the most of receiving the short straw, rebelling against what we could not change and pushing the boundaries of what was in our control to reshape.

Mostly, we were just trying to survive.

BAD APPLE

*Generational
bad apple falls from the tree
without core change.*

We often have little to no choice as children but to adapt to our surroundings, thus it can be easy to become a permanent product of our environment. We often fall into the natural cycle of generational pattern, morphing into the limitations by which we live.

As adults, we have increased ability to make our own choices. We can accept the path walked before us, or dig deep to find the strength and agility to forge a new way forward. I choose the latter.

I choose to break the chain.

BREAK THE CHAIN

*Reign
pretty in pink
think*

*big
breaking the chink
in the chain.*

The quest for perfection can be exhausting and can generate an abundance of judgemental pain rather than joy. Learning to appreciate one's body and mind can be difficult. For me, it was particularly hard, as I recall my mother always being overly critical, never once dishing out praise or giving out a hug. There was never a show of overt love. No matter how hard I tried, how well I did at school, how many certificates of merit I brought home, these were always met with stony silence at best, mocking sarcasm at worst.

Unconditional self-acceptance has been key to optimal wellbeing. I still strive to operate at my best, however, I am trying to retain some balance with keeping a healthy allowance for limitations, failures and flaws along the way. Over the years, I have made mistakes, said the wrong thing and made poor choices.

Haven't we all?

It's important to recognise the need to stop dwelling on past transgressions and replace these with continuous learning. I try to make a fresh start each morning. A long time ago I made a pact with myself to leave any residual Kryptonite from the prior day where it belongs – in the past – rather than drag remnants of negativity beyond another bright sunrise.

REVERSE ENGINEERING

Once
I was the struggle of my past
Until I past the struggle I was
Once

It took many years to mend the parentally inflicted wounds of demoralisation that broke through the Kevlar.

Evaluating toxic relationships can be an extremely tough and emotional exercise, but it is worth considering reducing contact with anyone who is poisonous in their behaviours towards you.

Everything is a choice. Whether to avoid people who make you feel bad about yourself or keep your self-esteem intact by hanging out with people who have your best interests at heart and you theirs.

Encourage others to celebrate uniqueness and treasure the value of every healed scar that makes us different. Surround yourself with like-minded people with positive voices who accept you as you are, including your shortcomings.

Many of us practised being perfect in childhood to meet other people's expectations, such as parents or teachers, but often these are harsh, unrealistic standards. We begin to be judged as children and often then become judgemental in adulthood. Yet it is impossible to actually be perfect. We all have days where we are irritable, get too little sleep, disappoint someone, forget something, are late or make a poor decision.

Try to avoid portraying a false persona to hide the cracks or to avoid seeming incompetent. There is nothing inherently wrong with you. Life is messy and challenges are peppered through our day-to-day existence.

You were never meant to be perfect, only perfectly you.

Human perfection is not the elimination of imperfections. It is the courage to accept your full wholeness, celebrating the richness of failures, fears and inconsistencies, all which give you personality, character and a unique edge. They are what make you real and relatable.

The harmonic of the universe is the wholeness that embraces differentiation rather than allowing the Kryptonite of perfection to hold us hostage in a radioactive environment.

STARGAZER MOMENT

There is no need
to prove
your worth
on this earth.

- Take stock of your own special combination of qualities, talents and abilities and recognise your self-worth.
- Know that you are worthy of being loved and cared for.
- Don't try to measure up to anyone else.
- Hold yourself to your own standards and avoid comparing yourself to others as everyone has a different path to take in life.
- Put yourself first sometimes.
- Refuel your batteries and indulge in self-care.
- Cease trying to be a people-pleaser who is always trying to satisfy others.
- Perfectionism makes it hard for us to connect with others and show up authentically because we're so focused on proving ourselves. Hang out with people who truly care about you and don't expect you to be perfect. They will appreciate you letting them see your vulnerabilities.
- Let the light flow into your cracks with appropriate openness and humility.
- Don't mistakenly assume that perfection is a prerequisite for ful-

filment of goals. The achievement of goals helps us to move forward, but do not get so hung up on what is lacking during the progress period that they become an impediment.
- Retire your inner critic as it no longer serves you any purpose. If it does resurface, see it as an opportunity to lend an ear to your internal dialogue, giving it the luxury of concentrated attention. Understand what inflames it, then accept the disapproving side of your nature and move on.
- Acknowledge the human frailty within our inherent paradox rather than seeing imperfections as an impairment.
- You are a complex being. Welcome your flaws and view them as gifts to transform into your true self.
- Grant yourself the gift of freedom to be you.
- Relish the wholeness of every inch of who you are.

Outline any unattainable standards you have set yourself. How can you adjust them to be more reasonable?

___

What are your quirks, flaws and insecurities hidden behind a facade? Can you allow others to begin to see the real you?

___

What was the last big mistake you made and can you use this to positive advantage?

___

___

___

___

___

___

IX
GALAXY

So here I am, with my feet firmly back on the ground, renewed energy abound, parallel worlds stranded, finally landed, right here, right now, without compartmentalism, ravishing existentialism as my mechanism to non-conform as I abandon Superwoman on Krypton. Arms open as I gulp and fill starved lungs with authenticity. Cracks shared, vulnerability bared, laser vision no longer impaired as I realise it's no longer necessary for us to feel the need to feed and breed duplicity. I am the dark side of the moon. The bright side of the sun. The sparkle of the stars. With the universe at one. I'm just one whole real deal and it's enough. We are enough.

This is my galaxy.

For many years, the creation of subconscious compartmentalising was a way to feel more in control of situations. I would divide up family, work and writing, breaking down tasks to be done at different points in the day. I would multitask, but within the constraints of each compartment, such as work tasks being managed alongside other work tasks.

The benefit of this approach was that I only had to think about one thing at a time. Creating virtual boxes meant each had my full undivided energy with nothing else competing for attention. There would be no conflicts pulling mental strings, vying for time, causing discomfort and unnecessary anxiety and tension. I decided to work on each individual task, large or small, and give that task the full force of my capabilities, without distraction, between set hours. For example, 6am-9am would be getting myself ready and the kids sorted for school, before travelling to the office. 9am-6pm would be used for work meetings and tasks. 6pm-8pm would be playing and bathing the kids. And 8pm-10pm would be quality time with my partner. However, it only left 10pm-6am to spend doing the things I wanted to do for me, like indulging in creative projects (hence the insomnia).

There was only one problem with juggling everything this way. I was always dropping at least one of the balls.

The launch of my first book, *Graffiti Lane,* a contemporary poetry collection made up of many poems I had penned over a few years, was a catalyst for change. My publisher, Karen Weaver, coached me on trusting the journey and embracing instinct and the inner sense of 'knowing'. She encouraged me to enjoy the hype as my gritty debut collection hit the bookshelves and to balance the madness with magical still moments of downtime. Her sound advice was supplemented by words of wisdom from my business mentor at the time, who also advised me to make the most of being in the public eye by allowing my authentic self to shine through in every forum, both at work and on the writing circuit.

The result was collapsing the walls between work, writing and family, and embracing a new blended approach to life.

After relocating to Sydney in January 2019, my daughter came into my new office in the city centre for the first time to see where I worked. She got to meet some of my team and assisted with a monotonous and momentous exercise that needed to be completed on a tight project deadline for an important client. She enjoyed every minute of being able to see where her mum worked and was a great little helper on a 'real-world' task.

As they got older, I began sharing my early writing drafts with both of my teenage children. They are now my biggest supporters, coming along to various literary events, as well as being my toughest critics. I invited colleagues, including my boss who was the CEO of the company I worked for at the time, to hear me speak about social issues and resilience at various writing events, something that was alien and incredibly personal at first. It felt awkward, like I was stripping back the skin and baring every inch of my vulnerable soul to people who had never seen that introspective side of me before. But it was also liberating to let the barriers down. To be vulnerable enough to share life's scars through poetry.

No more jumping between multiple personas. I merged my parallel worlds into one universe where I now have way more space to be just me, one person, and it's enough.

Accepting yourself completely and embodying your whole self means embracing authenticity. It's pointless striving to become someone you're not and maintaining a facade over time will very quickly become exhausting. It will strip you bare of what is real. Becoming your best self involves optimising all areas of your life to encourage growth. It is often a change of mindset, allowing you to develop confidence and promote your own positive thinking.

Authenticity commands self-awareness and demands we be true to our own personality. Our actions demonstrate genuine congruence with our own values, ideals, ambitions and desires, without succumbing to external pressures or overly worrying about being judged. However, this does not mean living life uncensored with a repertoire of uncontrolled behaviours. Developing restraint and acute listening skills, allowing other perspectives to come into play, is important, as being aware of what others feel forms a key part of effective interpersonal functioning.

Authenticity, for existentialists, is the degree to which actions are ingrained and sustained rather than influenced by tendencies to conform to the norms and expectations of the public world. Curious, balanced processing should solicit and welcome opposing viewpoints without jumping to foregone conclusions, keeping a strong moral code as a guiding compass.

Authenticity has both a bright and dark side.

Understanding your darker side is crucial to having a comprehensive rounded view of what is important to you in terms of social change and sustainability and is helpful in accepting faults and displaying relational transparency to take ownership of mistakes.

Emotions and qualities that we dislike about ourselves and fervently try to wish away are the traits that form our darker side, as opposed to poor choices or evil actions. They are the parts of yourself you would like to run away from, but it is impossible. Your darkest shadow will always follow you.

SHADOWS

We are the shadows of the night
escaping dark days
where the sun never shines
on our flight

We are the heat in the rays
of new energy generated
to change our plight
and fuel better ways.

Peeling back the onion layers and taking ownership of every part of yourself and accepting the good and the bad may take many years, if not a lifetime, to achieve. It is not a quick process.

One cannot simply self-declare authenticity and pat oneself on the back.

People develop their own perspective of others. As the world becomes more unstable and uncertain, they may judge more and expect an open book of truths. Face into this by being honest to yourself and others. Truth and vulnerability go a long way, not to encourage you to be a total loose cannon in bad behaviour, but to give you permission to be your authentic self.

It is not necessary to be the centre of attention with the world revolving around you. Sometimes it serves a far more important purpose to sit back, be yourself and let others shine.

Indeed, mammoth stars devour their fuel quickly. As a result, they generally last only a few hundred thousand years. Smaller stars burn fuel at a much slower pace so will shine for several billion years.

You can relax and glance up on the darkest night and watch every star appear to twinkle, however, in reality, stars do not actually twinkle. They just give the illusion of doing so from our perspective on earth, yet even though we are aware of this flaw in their make-up, they are no less beautiful to us.

ILLUSION

*Stars twinkling
create the inkling*

of illusion

*yet the blinking
is real fusion*

of mind and beauty.

To many onlookers, stars are something to be gazed at in wonderment. Basking in the twinkling of the stars brings a feeling of hope and joy.

We often also see shooting stars as a good omen to be wished upon, filled with the magical aura and ability to bring us luck and fulfil our dreams.

However, some also think of the fallen star as wayward, with no place to rest, and so they tumble from the sky. Ancient cultures believed fallen stars to be symbolic of missed opportunities since they are here one minute and gone the next.

Both shooting stars and fallen stars are meteors leaving a bright trail of light as they streak through the sky before disappearing into the darkness.

Stars are the light and they are the dark, yet they are one and the same.

STARGAZER MOMENT

*Don't fake it
until you make it,
just make it
authentic.*

- Embrace both the light and dark sides of yourself.
- Be open to the potential brought by continuous learning.
- Explore new experiences as they will create richness and are the seeds of growth in life.
- Avoid being a constant people-pleaser.
- Express your thoughts, feelings and views unapologetically yet considerately, simultaneously inviting in and respecting other perspectives.
- Give love and kindness indiscriminately as only by accepting others for being their authentic selves and giving them a helping hand can we help and accept ourselves.
- Look at challenging situations or mistakes that have occurred and try to identify the influence you have had.
- Take personal responsibility for actions and outcomes rather than pointing the finger at others.
- Do not be afraid to be the shooting star or the fallen star, for you have the ability to twinkle and shine your magical aura on others.

List your best traits and how you can use them to serve others and yourself better.

___

___

___

___

___

What are the qualities you believe to be your weaknesses?

___

___

___

___

What triggers the qualities you judge to be your worst? Next time you are triggered, pause in the moment, breathe slowly and only take action after you have had time to gather your thoughts.

_____

_____

_____

_____

_____

X
MILKY WAY

Now I'm Kelly Van Nelson, no longer the exhausted executive, poet and mum, instead I'm just me, re-energised in this galaxy filled with the brightest reality of no more complexity, only simplicity and efficiency in this eighth life. And I want to stay another day, ignoring the naysayers who say this milky way is just a step to pave the way to my ninth and final life, but although this might indeed be my plight, it's something I'll fight because I'm not quite ready to board that goodnight flight from this galaxy to my resting place beside papa in the afterlife.

In the beginning ...

There was an infinitely dense, microscopic ball of matter. Then, it all went bang.

According to contemporary cosmologists, the universe began with the Big Bang great explosion over 13.8 billion years ago. The universe began as a tiny, dense imperfection in the form of a fireball that exploded. Gravity gradually drew the matter together, giving rise to the first beautiful stars and the galaxies we see today.

According to the Book of Genesis, in the beginning God created the universe, the earth, sun, moon and stars in six days.

Whether you believe *'in the beginning'* was a cosmic Big Bang 13.8 billion years ago or a biblical phenomenon when God created earth 4.5 billion years ago, both point to the existence of an outside force that launched a universe which is now inhabited by perfectly imperfect humans.

We should not be fearful of imperfection, nor fearful of fear itself. Healthy fear gives us our armour to recognise and defend against danger, compels us to be alert and propels us to be action oriented rather than stagnant.

However, don't allow fear of life to be blown out of proportion, whereby it brings a thick, blinding fog, impeding your vision so you become solely focused on how others see you rather than having a line of sight on your chosen mission. You have to live life to its fullest potential in order to achieve yours.

UNAFRAID

I'm not afraid of dying.
I'm afraid of lying
to myself
while trying
to be someone else
who has never been alive at all.

We can so easily expend so much valuable energy trying to conform to what society considers traditionally acceptable that we avoid truly exploring our passions and exploiting our talents.

We forget to live.

Insecurities and paralysis by over-analysis stop us dead on the journey of adventure before setting us off down a more tortuous path of self-doubt. Imposter syndrome becomes the enemy that messes with the head.

Imposter syndrome can very quickly infect the mind, amplifying negativity, preventing the brain from recognising capabilities and achievements as real. High achievers with a shelf full of trophies and a wall filled with certificates are particularly at risk of believing they are undeserving of such accolades.

Superwomen the world over are offsprings of imposter syndrome.

We push ourselves to the upper limits, working harder than colleagues to cover up insecurities and measure up to self-inflicted personal standards. There is a tendency to think we might have achieved prior successes by sheer luck, when in fact we are some sort of phoney, so we stay late to earn our keep. And we take on more than is realistically achievable, then run solo because we are the expert and indispensable pair of hands that nobody can do without.

Perfectionism can frequently accompany imposter syndrome. As we strive to achieve utopia, the bar gets set higher and keeps getting raised until eventually the goals become unattainable. Even if we do make it over the finish line through being a whip-cracking control freak, our critique irrationally tells us that it was only a fluke.

Don't let the annoying voice in your head keep talking without an argument. If it is telling you that you don't have the education, skills, knowledge or experience, stand up to it.

Remind it of all that you have legitimately learned and strived to achieve over the years. Let it know that failure does not reflect inadequacy, it reflects human nature. Remind it you are a competent and skilled individual with an abundance of capability. Silence it with salient moments of the times you kicked ass and the success you fairly and squarely earned.

Become attuned to internal validation and convince imposter syndrome to doubt itself rather than letting it create doubt within you.

You are deserving of all that you have achieved.

IMPOSTER SYNDROME

If it were not for the laminated name tag
Stuck to my cubicle with Blu-tack
I would be a nobody

If it were not for burning the midnight oil
Leaving no stone unturned
I would still be barren of business cards

If it were not for practising debate in front of the mirror
To remove the quiver in my voice
I would never have influenced an outcome

If it were not for training my brain
To find creative ways to improve the status quo
I would forever be stuck in the way we've always done things

If it were not for building trust
With colleagues who share the load
I would not be able to carry the burden alone

If it were not for doing a good job
In consistently delivering on promises
I would not have a meaningful seat at the table

So, it's time to stop doubting myself every day
Pushing to the limit to keep the burning question at bay
Am I good enough?

While imposter syndrome may be an adversary that pops up every so often, self-motivation is a hero willing to fight for the cause whenever you need it.

If you look hard enough, self-motivation is around somewhere, readily available to allow you to tap into your own strengths to meet your goals rather than depend on others. It puts weaknesses into perspective, so you recognise them, begin to improve and resist letting them halt your hard work or hinder your plans.

Self-motivation is a confidence building block, driving you to go above and beyond. It will assist you in dreaming of endless possibilities and in finding either the satisfaction with your life or the courage and strength to change it. It is the weapon of destruction for imposter syndrome.

Don't be afraid of aiming high and of making mistakes along the way.

TARGET PRACTISE

If you aim for the stars
and miss
you might just land on the moon.

Don't mistake existentialism, where you are free and responsible as an individual for determining your own destiny, for existentialism perfectionism, the philosophical concept that life must be perfect in order to be worthwhile.

Existential perfectionism can manifest in different ways, making you feel constantly under pressure to strive for perfection in personal or professional life in order to be worthy of love and acceptance. It will result in you unfairly judging yourself as the harshest of critics.

Life is too short to waste a moment of it searching for validation elsewhere.

You truly are good enough.

HEY, UNIVERSE,

I am good enough.
I am good enough.
I am good enough.
I am good enough.
I am good enough.
I am good enough.
I am good enough.
I am good enough.
I am good enough.
I am good enough.
I am good enough.
I am good enough.
I am good enough.
I am good enough.
I am good enough.
I am good enough.
I am good enough.
I am good enough.
I am good enough.
I am good enough.

Be true to yourself and keep in touch with reality, with both feet firmly back on the floor. As children we learn from what is shown to us. These learnings provide the cement of our lifelong foundations. As adults, we learn only from the mistakes that cause a chip in this foundational cement that we notice, ponder upon, and either fix up or leave as a hole we are happy to walk past. Success is the result of remaining grounded, looking inwards and outwards at these cracks, to appreciate they are the basis on which our achievements are built.

Progress is having the courage to make decisions and the determination to take small positive steps each day to move forward in pursuit of a dream. This will lead you to long-lasting change for the future and convert dreams into reality.

This translates into simplicity, authenticity and actionable choices that carve a formidable streak of magic cutting through the night sky.

The Milky Way is the galaxy that includes the entire solar system.

It is the dark side of the moon and the bright side of the sun. It is several hundred billion stars that twinkle with illusion. It is the hazy and beautiful band of light seen in the night sky that cannot be distinguished by the naked eye.

It is every real and authentic part of you.

STARGAZER MOMENT

*We exist
because of an imperfection
which makes imperfection
perfection.*

- Simplify what is important and focus the fizz of your energy.
- Step out of your comfort zone and don't be afraid to make and own your mistakes.
- Find the optimism and ambition to drive forward and the doggedness and resilience to finish what you start.
- Use your initiative, be creative and believe wholeheartedly that you can do it – because you can.
- Define your goals and commit to them.
- Look for inspiration, start somewhere and say 'no' to perfectionism.
- Break down large goals into little steps.
- Never quit when you are frustrated. Always recalibrate after a setback and make decisions with a clear head.
- Surround yourself with supportive people, ask for help and offer it in return.
- Celebrate your achievements and those of others.
- Give imposter syndrome a stern talking to.
- Remind yourself that the universe is orderly and comprehensible.

Do not be afraid to push to the outer limits.
- Never stop stargazing until you find your Milky Way.

What are you going to tell imposter syndrome to shut it down?

_____

_____

_____

_____

What is the biggest lifelong dream you have?

_____

_____

_____

_____

What are the next steps you can take to get closer to it?

*… When did you last gaze
at the haze
of the Milky Way?*

The End.

MISSION ACCOMPLISHED

Many moons ago, when my first book came out, I wrote a long list of acknowledgements that seemed to span the breadth and depth of the universe and go on for an eternity.

I started as I mean to go on.

Thank you to Karen Weaver, Dylan Ingram and all at Making Magic Happen Press, for making my work sparkle that little bit brighter. You turned me into a shooting star.

A special mention to the TEDx organisers at Derry Londonderry Studio and the sponsors of my TEDx *Abandon Superwoman on Krypton* talk: Poetica, Story Room, WA Poets Inc, Suits or Shirts and MMH Press.

To everyone who took the time to watch my TEDx talk, read this book or stock it in your bookstores – you are my rocket fuel.

Heartfelt thanks to everyone who attended the 2023 Serenity Press Writers' Retreat at Crom Castle, Enniskillen, Northern Ireland. Much of this book was penned in the quiet moments between the inspiring country walks and eclectic evening talks.

Thank you to the 7th Earl of Erne, John Crichton, and Countess Harriet, for welcoming me into your beautiful home to scribble away in the most stunning of castle settings, and to Joan, Cynthia, Francis and Simon, for the impeccable hospitality.

Appreciation to Emma Weaver for keeping everything on track, including helping me get to the local Guinness tap to drink it dry and dance to Krom's tunes.

To the sisterhood that is Mickey Martin, Leah Martin and Sonee Singh, a joyful hurrah for the midnight author interviews, the laughter and the gin.

Peace Mitchell, Katy Garner, Dr Terari Trent and Sarah Ferguson, Duchess of York, gratitude for your ongoing commitment to supporting the women who are creating positive impact for others. Delighted to have picked up two bronze Women Changing the World Awards for Thought Leadership and Corporate Woman of the Year. We are a stronger force in driving change in society when we stand together.

A note of recognition also to the *Women's Network Australia* magazine and CEO, Cheryl Gray, who published several of my articles relating to improving female workforce participation in traditionally male-dominated industries. Let's keep playing our part in raising the profile of the women everywhere who are advancing in business.

Thanks to Sarah Atherton, Member of Parliament and Chair of the Women in Defence All-Party Parliamentary Group, and to all involved in the promotion of all women in the defence community. I extend the shout-out to the many like-minded changemakers I have met in the various parliamentary forums who are agitating the conversation to seek equality, fair opportunities and a safer work environment for women. We have come so far but the mission to create a future where societal and economic change is achieved by unlocking female potential is not over. Be louder!

Shaun, thanks for not letting a little thing like 15,000 km get in the way of Venus and for boarding the NASA rocket to visit me in the UK every once in a while.

Kayin, loved hanging out with you again for the second time at Crom Castle and seeing you shine with incredible talent and humility. You are the brightest sun and I am lucky to be your mum … see how that rhymes!

Imani, Europe became the best place on earth when we attempted rail navigation through several countries, with only the one little fifteen-hour hiccup in Germany. Cheers with a mulled wine to you being the next-gen amazing woman taking the world by storm. I am lucky to be your mum too … it's true. See how that also rhymes!

To all of the other incredible women out there, keep rewriting the rule book and chasing the mission. Now is the time to *Abandon Krypton,* and live life on your terms.

It was always your world.

Kelly Van Nelson is a contemporary author and poet from Newcastle upon Tyne. She lived in London, Edinburgh, Cape Town, L'Agulhas and Perth, before moving to Sydney, Australia. Her poems, short stories and articles have featured in numerous international publications, and she regularly appears on radio and television discussing current issues prevalent in society. She is represented by the Newman Agency.

Graffiti Lane, her powerful debut poetry collection, showcased at the London Book Fair and became an instant number-one bestseller, raising awareness and influencing change around bullying, mental health and suicide. *Punch and Judy,* her second bestselling poetry collection, puts the spotlight on domestic violence, generating much-needed conversation. Her third bestseller, *Retrospective,* explores the underbelly of urban life. She is also the author of *Rolling in the Mud,* a short story collection, and the curator of *Globalisation: The Sphere Keeps Spinning,* an anthology featuring several international poets. Her seventh book, a fiction novel, titled *The Pinstripe Prisoner,* was the 2022 winner of The Society of Women Writers NSW fiction award. Her books are frequently gifted to Hollywood celebrities, music icons and Academy Award winners.

Kelly is a 'KSP First Edition Fellowship' recipient and an AusMumpreneur 'Big Idea – Changing the World' gold award winner for her creative use of the literary word as an antibullying advocate. She is also a double-gold 'Roar Success Award' winner for 'Best Book' *(Graffiti Lane),* and 'Most Powerful Influencer'; 'Social Media Star' silver award winner, and bronze winner of the 'Making A Difference' award. In 2023 she was awarded bronze winner of two Women Changing the World Awards for 'Thought Leader of the Year' and 'Women in Corporate'. She is also a 'Telstra Businesswomen's Award' finalist and 'CEO Magazine Managing Director of the Year' finalist.

Kelly is the mum of two children, wife of her soulmate of almost three decades, TEDx speaker and managing director at a global organisation, where she is also the executive sponsor for gender equity.

In the spare time she doesn't have, you can find her mentoring underprivileged youths or hanging out on the open mic performing poetry around the world. In short, she is a juggler.

www.kellyvannelson.com

www.ingramcontent.com/pod-product-compliance
Lightning Source LLC
Chambersburg PA
CBHW020525080526
44583CB00013B/742